ADVANCE PRAISE FOR FENORRIS PEARSON AND

HOW TO PLAY THE GAME AT THE TOP

"Finally, a book that delivers exactly what it promises. As you read *How to Play the Game at the Top*, you quickly come to the realization that Fenorris Pearson is not cutting corners. He is providing a level of insight that takes most people their entire careers to understand. Read carefully, study hard, apply the principles of this book, and watch your career soar."

Richard J. Yeager, president,
Richard J. Yeager, LLC

"I know Fenorris Pearson. He is a consummate professional, a family man, and most importantly, genuine in everything that he does. He's been a corporate leader at some of the biggest companies in the world, and demands the attention of any entrepreneur, business leader, or success-oriented person looking for valuable insight on how to be an effective leader. This book will challenge your mind, as well as your perception of the leadership skills needed to be a difference-maker. For both young and old, don't just play the game—let Fenorris show you how to play it at the top!"

Hezekiah Griggs III,
multimillionaire media mogul, former teenage
entrepreneur wunderkind

How to Play the Game at the Top

THE 9 RULES FOR CONSUMMATE CORPORATE EFFECTIVENESS

Fenorris Pearson

B2
BOOKS

CHICAGO

Printed in the United States.

Library of Congress Cataloging-in-Publication Data

Pearson, Fenorris, 1968-

How to play the game at the top / by Fenorris Pearson, with Rusty Fischer.

   p. cm.

Summary: "Career guidance and advice for corporate professionals on how to reach and stay in top positions"--Provided by publisher.

ISBN-13: 978-1-932841-52-7 (hbk.)

ISBN-10: 1-932841-52-0 (hbk.)

1. Executives. 2. Career development. 3. Success in business. I. Fischer, Rusty. II. Title.

HD38.2.P43 2010

658.4'09--dc22

2010002544

10 12 13 14   10 9 8 7 6 5 4 3 2 1

B2 Books is an imprint of Agate Publishing. Agate books are available in bulk at discount prices. For more information, go to agatepublishing.com.

This book is dedicated to the loving memory of my mother, Katie Mae Pearson Sykes, who passed away in January 1996. My mother raised ten children—seven boys and three girls. I was the second to the youngest. Although we were extremely poor, she made me feel like I was the smartest and richest person in the world with her constant words of encouragement and her belief in me and what I could do and become.

She never let the fact that people talked about her and said that her kids would not be anything in life discourage her from wanting the best for all of her kids. She did everything within her means and power to ensure that I had a shot at making something out of myself.

My mother was taken by breast cancer. As many of you know, breast cancer is a disease that many women—and men—still fight to this day. I encourage all women and men who may have a history of breast cancer in their family to get checked out and conduct self-examinations. This is a disease that, if found early, has a high rate of full recovery. Although my mother was taken by breast cancer, her spirit and her sacrifices for me and our family are remembered and will never be forgotten.

All I am and all I will ever be is the direct result of a woman who worked two and sometimes three jobs to ensure that I had a chance to become the best I could be.

I love you, Mom, and miss you dearly!

Table of Contents

Acknowledgments

I'D LIKE TO THANK MY IMMEDIATE FAMILY—NICOLE, Fenorris Jr., Nicholas Q—who have endured many days of my traveling and working late nights to complete my book and continue to build my company, Global Consumer Innovation. Without your love and unconditional support, I would not be able to do what I do. I love you guys dearly!

I'd like to give a great big thanks to Marshall Goldsmith for believing in me and my vision for my book, and his willingness to write the foreword for this book. Marshall, I continue to be humbled by your generosity and willingness to help. Of all the many wonderful qualities you have as a professional, it is your giving and loving spirit that continues to impress me.

I'd like to give special thanks to Rusty Fisher: I couldn't have done this book with your assistance. You've been a trusted confidant and someone who believed in my vision when I approached you to help me write this book. I appreciate your help tremendously! I'd like to thank my father; my brothers Larry, Melvin, John Jr., Alfred, Ricky, and Maurice; and my sisters Carrie, Sharon, and Audrey (who has passed away) for their belief and constant encouragement to follow my dreams and goals throughout my life. I also want to thank my close friends and family members Maxine, Chris J., Adrian, Pia, Hezekiah,

Dennis P., Dr. Parker, Jeff O., Lawrence, Jerome N., Jonathan C., Hiriam H., Jamie P., Rick Y., Ron G., Alonzo M., Steve H., Ivan J., Gus, Curtis K., and Cliff C. for their support over the years.

Last, but certainly not least, I'd like to thank my management team at Ascendant Strategy Group, Raoul D., attorney Angela R., Carlos and Erica B., and my publisher, Doug Seibold, for their tough love and willingness to do what's right when representing my best interests in my business affairs.

Foreword

I HAVE BUILT A CAREER OUT OF HELPING EXECUTIVES reach higher, go farther, excel faster, and succeed longer in their own careers. One of the unwritten job skills of such a profession is to be "blunt without sounding blunt," or, to be "blunt without sounding (too terribly) blunt."

As an executive coach, this is something you have to master if you want to succeed. I haven't mastered it completely yet, but I know that if my clients are speaking to me by the end of the day, I must be doing something right.

To write a book like *How to Play the Game at the Top*, Fenorris Pearson also had to master the skill of being blunt without sounding (too terribly) blunt. He's done a fine job of letting the air out of the graduate school myth that an MBA is golden, out of the corporate wisdom myth that the status quo is the safest path, and out of the workplace myth that stepping over people is the surest way to the top.

This is not a book for wimps. It speaks truthfully from the perspective of a man who's been at the highest level of the game twice over, first at Motorola and later at Dell—two companies known for demanding the best from the best.

When I wrote *What Got You Here Won't Get You There*, I did so from my perspective as a coach who has helped great leaders like

Fenorris do what they do better. With that objective vision, I was able to write about leadership from the outside looking in.

Fenorris writes from the belly of the beast, telling it like it is in the nicest possible way. However, to share the message truthfully, Fenorris has some blunt words for his readers—words they'll be all the better for after reading.

- If you want to hear that life is great in corporate America, that your MBA is all you need to succeed, that you can still put in your 30 years and get a gold watch—plus a pension—upon retiring, then this is not the book for you. If, however, you want it straight from someone who's lived it, then this is the book for you.

- If you want to know what it's really like in that *Fortune* 100 company you've been dreaming of working for—how to navigate its waters, avoid its pitfalls, and overcome its inevitable obstacles—then this is the book for you.

- If you want to know how to craft a great résumé, forge alliances on the job, seek out a game-changing sponsor, and learn how to manage your peers—then this is definitely the book for you.

Finally, if you want to find out the nine rules for consummate corporate effectiveness, then this is the book for you.

It's not easy to play at the top. The people I work for, collaborate with, and learn from daily have tough, demanding, and challenging jobs. The rewards are high—but so are the expectations. You're here because you don't just want to play the game; you want to learn *How to Play the Game at the Top*.

—Marshall Goldsmith

Prologue

The Rules Are Different at the Top

THE WILL TO WIN IS ABOUT THE WILL TO PREPARE TO WIN!
—*Fenorris Pearson*

WALKING NERVOUSLY ONTO THE TARMAC FOR A midweek business trip, I was expecting to see the usual scene: various senior executives and their assistants milling about as they rolled their carry-on luggage over uneven pavement and waited impatiently for takeoff. What I saw instead was the man who had insulted me a few weeks earlier.

I had been interviewing senior executives in *Fortune* 100 companies for an upcoming report on organizational development. These were bigwigs, game changers, and experts in their fields, men and women, with all the right letters in their titles—CEOs, CFOs, VPs—and very few of them lower than the second or third in command of their respective divisions in their distinguished companies.

As one might imagine, it was intimidating work for me, the interviewer, but with my innate understanding, expertise, and passion for organizational development, and the interviewees' driving desire to make their company perform better, most of the executives I spoke with made the work as easy as possible.

After a long morning of Q & As, I was slated to interview a senior executive at a leading consumer communications firm. I was already dreading the confrontation. Mr. Peterson had a reputation for being extremely direct and to the point with his peers, let alone someone taking time out of his busy day to do organizational assessments.

I was not disappointed. Mr. Peterson came in late and, once seated, made no bones about the fact that he didn't want to be there in the first place. After a question or two, he said, point-blank, "This is incredibly stupid. Why do I even have to be here?"

At that point, I put my notebook down, looked him in the eye, and said, "Sir, you don't know me, and I don't know you, but I would appreciate it if you could tone it down and talk to me like I'm talking to you."

After that, the interview went on without a hitch. I got the information I needed and Mr. Peterson proceeded with his day. Throughout the interview, and throughout our eventual collaboration, not a single word was said about the confrontation—not then, not ever. After that meeting, Mr. Peterson didn't seem like a bad guy after all; in fact, he was great. Later in our relationship, I found out that the day we met, he had just gotten off a plane from India. He had only done the interview with me because he had heard great things about me, but was really in no mood to be talking after such an exhausting trip. If any of you have ever traveled to India, which is a lovely place, you will understand how mentally and physically draining a trip of that distance can be on your body and mental state.

But then a strange thing happened: Weeks later, I was invited by this very same man to an airstrip outside New York, Teterboro Airport, to talk about a "new strategy and vision" he had. "For whom?" I wondered, though I accepted the invitation without hesitation. When senior executives from *Fortune* 100 companies come knocking, you answer the door. Usually, however, such trips are hearty get-togethers, less talking and more playing, with plenty of executives and their assistants living it up outside the workplace.

Instead, at the airport that day, I saw Mr. Peterson and a chartered plane, both apparently waiting just for me.

I asked, "Where is everybody?"

Mr. Peterson gave an uncharacteristic smile and said, "It's just you and me, big fella." His reference to me as "big fella" was primarily because I stand 6'7" and am a former Division I student athlete.

None too eager to show my surprise, I boarded the plane and our trip was soon under way. After a few minutes at 30,000 feet, dinner was served, an elaborate affair with linen napkins, real silver, and a meal one would expect to get at a five-star restaurant, not aboard a moving vehicle.

After dinner, Mr. Peterson finally turned to me and said, "So, I guess you're wondering why I brought you here."

"Absolutely," I answered, swiveling in my leather seat to face him.

Mr. Peterson looked at me intently and said, "I figure if it's just you and I on board, out of the office, away from prying eyes and ears, I can really open up to you and, if you like what I have to say, great—but, if not, then it's just my word against yours."

Mr. Peterson wanted me on his team. He was offering me an opportunity to work for his company and taking the chance that I would be a good fit.

In other words, Mr. Peterson was offering to sponsor me. (Discussion of what a sponsor is will be presented later in this book.)

I have to admit, it was a seriously attractive offer. Despite his reputation for bluntness, directness, and demand for excellence, the man was a genius at corporate culture, and a creative genius. He was one of the smartest people I've ever been around in my life. He would later become one of my best friends in the world! He was a millionaire many times over—he knew everyone and anyone worth knowing—and his vote of confidence gave me instant entrée into that very exclusive world. But before our relationship became official, I needed to know one thing: "Why me?"

Mr. Peterson looked thoughtful before replying, "I didn't grow up with a silver spoon in my mouth either, Fenorris. I worked hard to make my own way in this business. Like you, I had a mother who made many sacrifices for my success today, and I've been fortunate to get a few hands up—but never a handout—along the way. Fenorris, I always promised myself that if I were ever in a position to help someone and could find a worthy candidate to sponsor who was true to himself and had grown up the way I did—intellectually well-rounded, a superior thinker, well-educated—that I would return the favor."

It was amazing to hear him say that. To look at the guy today, it seemed that he'd grown up in a far different world from where I came from, but...

He did not, in fact, grow up rich.

He was a hard worker. He grew up in meager circumstances, wore jeans, and, while he did end up at Ivy League schools, it was through hard work and meager circumstances, not some trust fund legacy or letter of recommendation from an influential family friend. It was hard to believe, but true just the same. Here was a guy—custom-made pin-striped suit and suspenders, the private jet, the gourmet meal, the titan of industry, lord of home and manor—and he had grown up just like me?

He'd built a future for himself, but now, in his position, he felt uncomfortable around some of his peers. Many of them shared identical backgrounds, educational experiences, and had even been college roommates. Their background was not his background, but, amazingly, mine was.

To think this man had more in common with me than the titans of industry didn't just give me the hope that I could one day be in his position—it gave me the confidence to know I was already on that well-worn path.

He didn't have to do this for me. He didn't have to reach out to me and give me a handhold up to the top of the game. The fact that he took the time to do this for me didn't just change which level of the game I was at—it changed my life, and I will be forever grateful to him and, of course, God.

What Got You Here Won't Get You Anywhere!

For some time now, the modern workplace has been morphing, shifting, and evolving into a very different place from your grandfather's or mother's job site. Change comes so quickly, policies evolve so rapidly, and climates shift so dramatically that even what you learned in your undergraduate classes, let alone while obtaining your MBA in grad school, might already seem outdated by the time you find yourself in that first cubicle.

Gone are the days of 30-, 20-, or even 10-year careers at the same company. Today, leapfrogging from job to job, and even company to company, isn't just unheard of—it's standard operating procedure. According to the Bureau of Labor Statistics for 2005, "the voluntary turnover rate across the board in 2009, this past year in the U.S. was 20.2 percent."

Productivity is down but expectations are up. Gen Xers and now members of Generation Y expect more return for less work and, worst of all, act accordingly. According to Virginia Prescott of New Hampshire Public Radio, "A Microsoft survey of more than 38,000 people worldwide found that workers, by their own admission, average only three productive days per week."

Meanwhile, even as employee standards continue to decline executive expectations of those very same employees continue to rise; they want more productivity, respect, and responsibility, not less.

And yet, employers themselves are getting bad report cards from the people directly under them. According to recent research from Delta Road, a Denver-based career coaching firm, "… Eighty-one percent of 700 employees surveyed classified their immediate supervisor as a 'lousy manager,' up a third from sixty-three percent just two years ago. Another sixty-nine percent said their boss had 'no clue' on what to do to become a 'good manager.'"

So how does one bridge the great divide between what executives want and what employees are willing to give? How does one excel in a climate of both employee- and employer-created mediocrity?

How can you create a passionate, purposeful career for yourself in a culture of leapfrogging hitchhikers and insufficient motivators? And how can you leapfrog yourself from reporting to a bad boss to *being* the boss?

For starters, you must first understand one golden rule.

The Rules Are Different at the Top

Today I am the CEO of Global Consumer Innovation, Inc. (www. globalconsumerinnovation.com), or GCI. Before starting my own company, I was the vice president of global consumer innovation and global capability for Dell Inc., a *Fortune* 50 company with revenues of more than $60 billion. While at Dell, I had a senior leadership role and responsibility for more than 300 employees in Europe, Asia, and the Americas. I also developed the skill capabilities of Dell's consumer business sales, retail, and service functions.

Before joining Dell, I was vice president for global organizational for Motorola, Inc., a global telecommunications leader with revenues of more than $40 billion. My responsibilities encompassed major strategic acquisitions, process reengineering efforts, and development of the company's performance management process. Before joining Motorola, I worked at Corning Consumer Products, one of the leading household products companies in the world, as an executive in organizational development with brands like Corningware, Oxo, Corelle, and Chicago Cutlery. I had a sponsor who gave me my first shot at a senior executive role and started me on my way to the top. He taught me about maintaining your honor and values in the midst of corporate giants and greed, while not letting money and ego ruin you.

My positions at Dell and Motorola made me one of the youngest VPs of a *Fortune* 50 company ever—and both went on my résumé before I turned 40.

So let me be the first to tell you that I have seen the future of corporate America, and not only is it cutting edge, it's razor sharp. It is not your grandfather's career and it's not even your father's career; what's happening to the modern workplace is like nothing we've ever seen before and to stay competitive, let alone prosper, you will need help. And not just of the traditional variety. Unfortunately, what worked for Mom and Dad won't work for you. What propelled former generations to become titans of industry will barely get you in the door today, let alone to the top of your chosen profession.

People say, "What got you here won't get you there," but I say, "What got you here won't get you anywhere!" Now is the time to jettison what you think you know, wipe the slate clean, make room for an entirely new business paradigm, and face the facts: to play at the top, you need a whole new set of rules.

I wish your MBA, your letters of recommendation, and your dreams were enough to get you to the top. I really do. I wish your Ivy League degree, your stellar GPA, your well-rounded résumé, your impressive performance record at work, your standing on the succession-planning chart, your spit-shined shoes, and your go-get-'em attitude were all it took to succeed in this day and age. But this isn't that kind of book.

This isn't the kind of book that purports the great American lie, the unkind—and untrue—fabrication that says you can become whoever you want to be in whatever field you choose to go into just because you put in 40 hours a week and don't go five miles over the speed limit during your daily commute.

Bad careers really *do* happen to good people. Coworkers turn out to be "frenemies," sometimes even enemies. That promotion often goes to someone far less talented—but much more related to the boss—than you. These are the facts, as hard as they are to swallow.

If you've been around the corporate culture long enough, you already know that I speak the truth. If you're new to the game, then consider me that well-meaning uncle, that mentor, that voice of reason that gently but firmly urges you to "wake up and smell the coffee."

This is the book that is sometimes hard to swallow but absolutely vital to your success in today's modern, connected, and network-heavy workplace. Yes, you will need your great GPA, your graduate degree (eventually), your sterling-silver cuff links, your ironclad work ethics, and your entrepreneurial spirit internally or externally. But in addition to all that you will need a firm understanding of what it means to play the game at the top as an executive or an entrepreneur owning or starting your business.

Going Up? These Nine Rules Will Take You There

For my entire life, I have strived to be better. Through hard work, spirituality, and passion and a series of happy coincidences, powerful connections, and habitual performance, I have reached the top and have no intention of leaving anytime soon!

- How did I get there so quickly?
- How did I stay there?
- And what can you do to get to the top?

I won't say the journey was easy (far from it, in fact), but it *is* possible. Please don't think I'm trying to discourage you or bench you before the game even gets started—far from it. But unlike Little League, where everybody gets to play regardless of whether they put the glove on the correct hand or know where left field is, this is the real world, and everything is performance based.

But even performance isn't always enough. Over and above your performance, your sales figures, your great marketing ideas, or your social skills, there is a series of unwritten rules that everyone at the top knows, but few are willing to share. These are the rules I followed to find success and that will help you become a top performer and, ultimately, a consummate executive:

- **Rule #1:** How to Keep Your MBA from Becoming DOA
- **Rule #2:** The All-Inclusive Résumé—What Really Counts!
- **Rule #3:** Get Sponsored to Change Your Career Overnight
- **Rule #4:** Dream Big—They Can't Measure What's in Your Heart
- **Rule #5:** Forging Alliances—Popular Vote vs. Electoral Vote
- **Rule #6:** Managing Your Peers and Keeping Your "Enemies" Close
- **Rule #7:** Green—The Only Color They See!
- **Rule #8:** Corporate Winning
- **Rule #9:** It's Not Just About Getting to the Top, But How You Play the Game

The Only Rules That Matter

I am a big believer in not just giving, but giving back. I have been helped so often and by so many on my own personal climb to the top that I would be remiss if I didn't reach down from time to time and help out wherever and whenever I can. One of the ways I try to give back is to speak widely on the topic of making it to the top.

One day I could be speaking at a Rotary Club or chamber of commerce, the next an Ivy League school, or, just as often, a middle school. People everywhere want to get to the top—that's what's so great about America! But we have been so deluded by fortune-cookie wisdom and whitewashed corporate history that too many of us believe that simply showing up earns us the corner office.

I believe that although what I have to say isn't always well-received, it *is* a step in the right direction. The sooner you know what it takes to get to the top, the sooner you can start climbing in the right direction.

Every time I speak at a community center, state college, corporate luncheon, or charity event, inevitably a handful of recent graduates and entry- to mid-level employees corral me to ask the same basic question: "I've got the MBA, my résumé is impeccable, and I've done the internships—why haven't I been hired/promoted yet?"

What I tell them isn't always met with a great reception: "Don't be disappointed. Don't be a victim. Don't think graduate school, private school tuition, or all those years you may have already spent on the job were a waste—they weren't. Yesterday is over; this is a new day. Stop complaining about what's *not* good enough and realize what is."

You can deny me and go on doing what you've always done, or you can believe me and do what you need to do. Either way, the choice is up to you. My feeling is this: I wish someone had told me sooner rather than later that life isn't always fair; that way, I would have responded accordingly much, much sooner.

The bad news is that the climb will be a lot tougher than you thought it was.

The good news is that there is always—always—room at the top for the candidates who follow these nine previously unwritten rules to getting there. It's almost like a secret language spoken among C-level executives across the country; and once you know its alphabet, you can speak that language and join the club. Until then, you'll always be on the outside looking in. The reality is that an Ivy League education, spotless GPA, impeccable performance record at work, and high and tight haircut will only take you so far.

Bring Your Career into Focus

Success is a matter of focus; paying attention to the right thing versus the wrong thing is often the only difference between success and failure. So quit focusing *outside* yourself on the external trappings of corporate success and realize what specific and unique *inner* qualities you bring to the job that can and will make you a consummate executive.

People often consider success as an event, but game-changers know that success is not won in major victories, knockouts, or happy Hollywood endings but by inches, degrees, and hours.

Don't wait for magic to happen, for others to notice you, or for the workplace equivalent of the big Lotto win. Instead, make your career a habit—and habitually strive to improve. No one will give you anything. You must earn everything. Know that life is not fair and move on. Know that corporate America isn't a democracy!

Remember that some of today's most brilliant, fascinating, polarizing, successful, and iconic success stories never got an MBA. For that matter, many of them never even finished college. Men like Bill Gates, Steve Jobs, and my own former leader at Dell, Michael Dell, aren't ashamed to say that they did not finish college. They knew a degree didn't define them any more than a job description or GPA.

Here's the skills that really matter:

- Performance
- Loyalty
- Results
- Passion
- Dedication
- Commitment

None of them can be measured by a scorecard. Instead of keeping score via the amount of credentials on your office wall or the number of letters that come after your name, focus on the fundamentals and commit to them entirely.

Finally, believe in the power of your own dreams. Work hard, but love what you do. Even if your first job is in the mail room, treat that mail room like it's your first day in the corner office and you will perform accordingly. What's more, people—the right people—will notice. The rules may be different at the top, but how will you ever know if you don't play by them?

Rule #1

How to Avoid Your MBA Being DOA

ONE OF THE FIRST THINGS YOU NEED TO KNOW TO play the game at the top is that your MBA (or, for that matter, any graduate degree you may have received during the educational phase of your career) is not necessarily a means unto itself but is in fact merely a tool for success.

To play the game at the top—to become consummate executives— you need to stop thinking of the once-coveted MBA degree as the endgame and instead consider it part of what I call your "employment pyramid" for reaching your ultimate goals.

When it comes to proving your worth or value to the decision makers at any company, during any phase of your career, make sure that your MBA is never at the top of your personal selling points.

When you are actively seeking employment, a promotion, or anything you want that pertains to your job, you need to start thinking in terms of an employment pyramid.

The Employment Pyramid:
How to Get to the Top by Starting at the Bottom

What is an employment pyramid? Simply put, it's a thought organizer or visual tool for how you prioritize your skill sets, attitude, education, and personality—anything that pertains to the new job or position.

Every skill is important; every grade, degree, connection, award, recognition, or tool will help get you to the top. However, let's face facts: some skills are simply more important than others.

It's a little like making a salad. Some salads are fancy, some are plain, some are filling, and some are dainty, but this much can be said of all salads—each is created uniquely. Some use Bibb lettuce, others field greens, others baby spinach. You can have as many toppings as you want, and all can be quite tasty, but every salad begins with a few basics: greens, other vegetables, and, of course, salad dressing. Then each salad gets its own layers of additional ingredients. One layer of the salad can affect the others.

Much like salads, pyramids have layers. Specifically, pyramids have bottoms, middles, and tops, but one section can't exist without the other, so this isn't an issue of priorities. In other words, you need the bottom of your pyramid to form a solid foundation for the top— and you need the top of your pyramid to cap off your foundation.

It's a great way to think about your MBA because in an employment pyramid, the degree is neither at the top or the bottom—it is squarely in the middle. So in a résumé, for instance, your MBA shouldn't be the first line; in conversation, it shouldn't be the lead topic. If you put your MBA in the middle of your accomplishments, it actively makes you do, find, use, or say something to put on top of it.

So, for instance, if your undergrad degree and extracurricular activities are at the bottom of your employment pyramid, and your MBA is in the middle, what goes on top? Community involvement? Previous job expertise? Glowing references? Putting your MBA in the middle of your accomplishments makes you look at it differently; and then other people will, too.

Don't Fall for the MBA Hype

MBA grads often think they're halfway home when they receive their diploma—and that securing their first corporate job is the second half of the solution. Don't misunderstand me; getting a degree at any level is a great accomplishment. What I tell people when I give lectures across the country is that between the beginning of your career and the end, you will need many tools to achieve your goals. You'll need to learn many lessons, form many relationships, and develop many skill sets. Ultimately, you'll learn that your MBA is just one of the many tools you'll need to play the game at the top.

Why do I mention this potentially bad news here, in my first rule for playing at the top? It's simple: The sooner you realize that life exists beyond the MBA or any degree after high school, the sooner you'll embrace the rest of the rules in this book.

It's a little like believing in Santa Claus. As a kid, that worked fine: your parents brought you presents each year from Santa, and you believed in him. They knew the score—you didn't—but it was okay because you were a kid and everything worked out. But now the veil has been ripped back, you've seen the wizard behind the curtain, and unfortunately, you've learned that Santa isn't real.

Think of corporate America as being no different. Knowing that your MBA isn't enough now is going to help you later on when you do those things that need to be done to build a career around your MBA rather than depending on your MBA entirely.

I was very blessed and fortunate to achieve success in three of the biggest companies in the world at a VP level before I was even 40 years old—first at Motorola, quite a feat in itself, and later at Dell and Corning Consumer Products.

Now, working for one *Fortune* 50 company is often the pinnacle of a person's career; some would argue that was playing at the top. And it is. But playing at the top for two of this country's premier corporations gives me twice the expertise to say what goes on behind closed doors at two of America's biggest game-changers.

These are the kinds of corporations that people talk about when they say they want to "play at the top." The people you meet in such companies, the teams you collaborate on, the projects you complete, and the success you achieve—truly if you can make it here, you *can* make it anywhere. And if there's one thing I've learned, it's that every successful person in every successful corporation brings his or her own arsenal of talents, tools, and resources on which to draw. For some, it's absolutely their MBA, their degrees, their educational component. For others, however, it's their street smarts, their common sense, or their analytical approach while the rest of the office is getting emotional. No tool is more important than any other; they all have a job to do in the modern workplace.

So, your MBA is no longer the top of the game but, instead, a helpful tool you can use to win the game *if* you choose to back it up with all the other traits, tools, and skills you'll need to succeed.

The point is not to knock any MBA or undergraduate programs, as it's absolutely vital to have a solid educational core to enter corporate America or to be a thriving entrepreneur these days— but it's vital as a part of the journey and not the destination itself.

Ten Things an MBA Is

What will an MBA get you? Again, let me just say that my hat is off to anyone who can get, let alone capitalize on, this stellar educational achievement. An MBA is an auspicious beginning to an accelerated career, but it is just that: a beginning.

Here are ten things an MBA is:

1. A stepping stone: Every path begins with a single step, and few steps are as big, as daunting, or as rewarding as getting your MBA.

2. A benchmark: Many corporations have a basic standard of excellence or series of requirements that they tick off on a checklist when going to hire a new candidate; an MBA is one of those items most corporations look for, if not downright require, in any new candidate for employment.

3. An example of your dedication to excellence: What an MBA tells people is that you can dedicate yourself to doing something special and, ultimately, bring that goal to its fruition.

4. A milestone in your educational development: When we take a class, we expect to get a grade. When we enter high school, we expect to graduate. And when we go to business school, we want to come out with the highest degree available—the MBA.

5. An achievement to be recognized: Companies the whole world over recognize the value of an MBA as an achievement to be recognized, reveled in, and, quite often, rewarded.

6. A sign that you can set a goal and reach it: Goal setting and achieving are two skills every corporation covets. When you set a high educational standard for yourself and reach it, companies sit up and take notice.

7. A step in the right direction: Your MBA tells people where you are headed—straight to the top!

8. An opportunity for bigger and better things: The more prepared you are to play the game, the better your chances are for getting to the top. An MBA gives you a leg up on the competition and a foot in the door.

9. An accomplishment to be proud of: Few educational achievements are as prominently recognized and rewarded as the MBA. You are to be commended.

10. An intermission before the big show: Finally, an MBA is that calm before the storm: a chance to stay in school a little longer, perfect your game, and prepare for the next phase of your employment evolution, that first corporate job.

Ten Things an MBA Isn't

While an MBA is the crowning achievement of many an academic success story, it isn't the guarantee it once was for corporate success. Following are ten things an MBA isn't:

1. A finish line: You are not done. Much learning and many experiences and expectations await you on your journey to the top. Thinking of the MBA as your finish line just makes you stop learning sooner, and corporate success is all about lifelong learning.

2. A sure thing: To think you are a shoo-in for a job because of your MBA whitewashes the reality that you will be up against many varied applicants who also have an MBA. What you do to augment your graduate degree with additional awards, achievements, recognitions, and skills will truly determine whether or not you get that job or promotion.

3. A price cap: To stop at your MBA limits your own career path—not to mention your earning potential—and tells potential employers that your goals only extend so far. To play at the top, your hiring personnel will need to see that you're ready to go to any lengths to get there.

4. A reason to quit growing educationally or professionally: The danger in giving too much credence to an MBA is that you don't give enough weight to *what happens next*. Employers want to know that you can think on your feet, adapt, and respond accordingly to any situation, not rest on your laurels. If you stop growing after you get your MBA, your occupational education is only half complete.

5. A sign that you're the right person for the job: If playing at the top is a business suit, then your MBA is like a stylish, classic, fitted blazer. Sure, you look the part and will get a second glance, but if you're not wearing any pants (i.e., bringing any additional skills to the table), no matter how great your blazer looks, you're still going to show up only half-dressed.

6. A lock: If you've ever seen an underdog team come from behind to beat a team that has them outscored and outplayed,

you have seen the team that thought they had a lock, a shoo-in, brought down by its own overconfidence. Be the underdog, not the team that thought it had the victory locked in.

7. A ticket straight to the top: You can't get on the bus without a ticket but not every ticket takes you the same distance. Make sure you don't stop before you reach your final destination by believing that your MBA is a ticket straight to the top.

8. An excuse to stop learning, growing, and achieving: Resting on their laurels never got anybody past their earliest accomplishments. Those who play at the top are lifelong learners; every degree, accomplishment, bonus, raise, or promotion is a step toward the finish line, not the finish line itself.

9. A guarantee: There are no guarantees in business, let alone in the human resources department.

10. A reason to get comfortable: Players at the top know that business isn't a dead thing but a living thing. It doesn't just sit there playing by the rules. It grows and evolves and is always, ever changing. To think that once you've gotten your MBA you're in some way "done" is to deny the ever-changing nature of business, which is in a constant state of flux

An MBA Is Not the Gold Standard It Once Was

As we all know by now, years ago, the MBA was *the* gold standard for excellence in education. It used to automatically grant a person success—success, of course, as it relates to achieving an executive-level role in corporate America whether it be a mid-level management position or the director or vice president title.

Unfortunately, that simply is no longer the case. It's really important that you understand how to navigate your career inside the corporation once you get there, whether or not you have your MBA. Some people think that just because they have an MBA, they should automatically be at the top of the game. Other people with

MBAs think that performing well or having the best performance scores will automatically lead to success. Again, these qualities and traits are part of the recipe you'll need to succeed but are not signs of success unto themselves.

It's a little like the quarterback handing you the ball just before the end zone and saying, "Now all you have to do is run it in." Everything is in place—the defenders are too far downfield to catch you (within reason, of course), and you've got the ball in your hand and a clean shot for scoring a touchdown. But if all you do is stand there with the ball in your hand and don't take the next few steps to get you into the end zone, you are giving up before you even get started. By the same token, your MBA is just the handoff: what you do with the next few steps of your career makes all the difference.

Many students believe they have already succeeded just by getting an MBA, and they're right. They have achieved a notable (educational) distinction and are more than deserving of accolades. However, early success is only a *sign* of future success—not the definition of success itself.

What gets you success these days is really, completely, and with an open mind understanding how to play the game at the top. Given the fact that companies have to be much more efficient and effective regarding how they leverage their resources these days, they need more than just your MBA to predict future success.

The Tenth Candidate: A Recipe for Success

The starting line for new employee candidates has been moved back indefinitely. Nowadays, if 10 people apply for a current job in corporate America and nine of them have MBAs and one doesn't, no longer is the one without that additional degree automatically kicked out the door and sent packing.

Instead, modern corporations recognize that academic success is only one predictor of future success; they will grill and question this tenth candidate much the same way they will grill and question you and, if his or her answers are what they're looking for—or even indicative of future success—that candidate will still get called back for a second interview, maybe even get the job, all without an MBA.

These days the person *without* the MBA may just be a smidge ahead of those nine other candidates, if only for the fact that he or she will have to bring a little more to the table to prove himself or herself worthy of the job.

In other words, put yourself in that tenth candidate's shoes. Let's say you're going to work for a *Fortune* 100—maybe even a *Fortune* 50 company—and you know only the best and brightest have made it this far. In fact, you're absolutely, positively certain that nine out of every ten candidates will have an MBA. So don't you think, given the fact that you don't have an MBA, you're going to overcompensate by trying twice as hard as everybody else there; by being twice as prepared as those nine other candidates; and by bringing your A++ game to every question, every response, every gesture, and every moment of eye contact? Absolutely the tenth candidate is going to come prepared, and then some—and oftentimes, preparation is just the edge he or she needs.

Meanwhile, I've seen many candidates with an MBA walk into an interview supremely confident that the job was already theirs, only to walk away crushed that they didn't make it past the initial interview, let alone get called back to sign their W-2 forms the next morning.

Modern companies are faced with a much larger question beyond the MBA these days: How do you leverage the talent that you have in order to achieve success for the company? So regardless of how academically successful you have been at Harvard, Yale, or elsewhere, once you're on the job you *still* have to perform; you *still* have to produce. You have to get results. Your MBA helps get you in the door, but it will no longer automatically get you that big promotion that you're looking for.

What Does an MBA Really Mean to Corporate America?

Whether you are reading this book during good times or bad, during a recession or a rebound, or a bubble or a bust, the fact that you are reading it at all assumes that you realize how tough it's gotten in corporate America these days, and you need an extra play or two to get you to the top. Perhaps you're already on the inside and are facing new challenges to your job growth; maybe you're entry level and looking at a long climb or even just hoping for a job to get one foot in the door. Chances are, wherever you fall on the scale of success, you've discovered that corporate life is no longer the "sure thing" it used to be.

The selection process is tougher, for one thing. No longer are you simply judged on your educational prowess but on a host of other skills as well, from social to political, from how you handle stress in the workplace to how you handle others.

Indeed, the new reality of corporate life is that once you're in, great; now you hit the giant "reset" button and start all over again. In other words, you're no longer ahead of the game, because now you're on the same level with everyone else.

For people coming into corporate America in this climate, the MBA is a valuable step in the right direction, but those who are already in the organization shouldn't feel threatened if they don't have those three little letters in their résumé.

If an MBA gets you in the door, it stops there; you have to take it to the next level based on your own personality, skill sets, and level of performance. You have to show how you're going to use that MBA to move forward. You are on your own to prove yourself. It's an even playing field once you get inside.

Here is what your MBA means to corporate America: basically, that you have the capacity to achieve a certain level of success. Here's what corporate America knows that you may not (yet): having the capacity to achieve and achievement are two totally different things.

An MBA does not instantly give you success. What an MBA does is allow you the ability to be in the running to achieve success. I want to be very clear and very candid here: At the end of the day, you will see many executives in corporate America that don't have their MBA or, in some cases, even an undergraduate degree.

David K. Zwiener, an executive vice president at Hartford Financial Services Group Inc., agrees. Quoted in a March 2006 article for *BusinessWeek*, Zwiener explained, "It [an MBA] opens that first door for you. After that, it's up to you." In fact, according to *BusinessWeek* magazine, "research has found that fewer than one out of three executives who reach those lofty heights do so with the help of an MBA."

These hard statistics prove what my own experience has taught me throughout the years; the top players don't all come from the same background, or the same schools or have the same degrees. No, what the players at the top have in common is that they know how to play the game and have the innate skills it takes to survive and dominate while doing what others can't. Those are the skills I'm trying to teach you in this book; those are the rules I'll be sharing with you throughout.

When I see a recent MBA grad, or a grad student, realize that this degree doesn't give "instant access" to success, I'm often reminded how unprepared they really are for the current reality of the modern corporate workplace. Some MBA students are crushed and caught off balance when they see people who already have MBAs not progressing at the rate of success they would like to have. It's almost painful to watch. And the reason behind that disconnect between reality and perception is that they have not figured out yet that it's beyond just getting that good performance score that translates into success these days—it's effectively navigating your career.

An MBA allows you the ability to be in line for the success most MBA students dream of having before they get out of college—

undergrad or graduate. What an MBA grad needs to know is not necessarily how to get an MBA but why it's important to have an MBA. It helps you, but it does not automatically guarantee you the ability to achieve success. The sooner you realize this fact, the earlier you can put your MBA into perspective and start building up those additional skills you need to round out your employment pyramid.

I have given this message to hundreds of MBA students. I have counseled and coached them and just looked into their eyes, students from some of the biggest schools in the world—such as Harvard, Yale, Wharton—and these students wondered why they were not progressing in their careers like they thought they would, even with an MBA from these hallowed institutions.

I don't want you to share that same sense of disappointment I see all around the country, so what I'm trying to do here is help you navigate your career *before* you get inside corporate America to really help you understand how you're going to achieve success.

The VP Without an MBA

You may be surprised to learn that I don't have an MBA. Again, I want to convey to you that there's nothing wrong with earning an MBA. All I want to dispel is this notion that an MBA automatically ensures that success is going to come about, regardless of your performance or, in many cases, lack thereof.

I do have a master's degree, just not an MBA. I have a master's degree of science in organizational development.

Becoming a Consummate Executive

What you need to know is that the goal is not to be a consummate student, which is what, in effect, gaining your MBA does for you. School is out, and now the real work begins. What modern corporations want now are consummate executives, and that is what this book is going to teach you.

A consummate executive does the following:

- *Knows the rules and plays by them*: Every company has its own rule book. Unfortunately, you can't download these books from the Internet or ship them overnight from Amazon.com; they don't even hand them to you as you walk in the door on your first day as an employee. In fact, most of these corporate rule books are completely unwritten. They are like a secret code that you must decipher from day one on the job and learn throughout your tenure with the company. For instance, dress code is a common unwritten rule in many corporations. Even if you ask someone in HR what the formal dress code is, he or she will simply tell you "business casual." But a savvy employee knows that's really code for, "Wait and see for yourself." And so you must learn who wears what, what's appropriate and what's inappropriate, and what is respected and what is not. It's political, it may even be petty, but it's important to those who matter, and so you must play by those unwritten rules if you wish to follow a smooth path to success. Knowing the rules is only half the battle—playing by them helps you to the top. Knowing what rules to play by is critical to your success, but only if you actually follow them.

- *Can adapt when the rules he or she learned in college don't translate to success in corporate America*: A consummate executive knows that what he or she learned yesterday is only good for so long. You can't think you've learned all the rules, and that's that. The rules change every day. It's a little like being on a movie set and thinking you're prepared because you memorized your lines last night. Every day, little changes occur that force you to learn a new scene of dialogue or maybe even unlearn what you've memorized and start over. The actor who assumes work is over once the lines are memorized is

destined for daily surprises. Likewise, consummate executives
know that change is the only constant, that the rules they
learned yesterday are merely guidelines for what they will
learn today, let alone tomorrow. Success is a moving target,
be it academic success, social success, or professional success.
Now is the time to learn a whole new set of rules to play your
way to the top.

- *Understands that the days of having an MBA equal instant
  success are long over:* Remembering that an MBA is only part
  of the DNA for success sets consummate executives apart
  from regular success stories. Consummate executives are made
  of heartier stuff—they are the sum of many, many parts, of
  which the MBA is only one.

- *Knows that success is not only performance- or academic-based
  but has to do with how one navigates the land mines of corporate
  America:* Every company is fraught with obstacles and land
  mines that threaten to derail your success, and you must not
  only avoid but overcome them. Throughout this book, you
  will be introduced to some of them, including office politics,
  colleagues as enemies, and a host of other challenges.

- *Understands that the rules change every day:* Know that the
  rules change every day, that supervisors are moody, that teams
  aren't static, that client demands rule the day, and that every
  day, without fail, the rules change. Consummate executives
  embrace change—maybe not naturally but, over time, they
  are faced with it so often that they learn to make it their
  comfort zone. Really, they have no choice. If you can't adapt
  to change, if you can't welcome it, expect it, covet it, and
  use it to your advantage, you'll never make it to the top—let
  alone stay there very long.

- *Is comfortable operating with only 80 percent of the facts:* To
  become a consummate executive, you must remember that

you will never have all the facts. Knowledge is the fuel by which modern corporations are run; facts are the building blocks of knowledge. So understand that, to many people, facts are things to be savored, favored, and doled out accordingly. Some facts are hidden on purpose, some are kept private for personal reasons, and some not even the higher-ups know! Corporate America thrives on secrecy, and you must get comfortable with making fast decisions with only 80 percent of the facts.

In short, a consummate executive thinks on his or her feet, assesses each situation on an individual basis, and responds accordingly. You did not waste time if you got your MBA—no doubt you learned many valuable skills in the time it took you to get that degree.

On the other hand, don't be discouraged if you didn't get your MBA. The playing field is still level; the starting line is the same for MBA and non-MBA grads. Right now, in this day and age, you are both on an even playing field; it's what you do next that matters.

Will You Get a Seat on the Bus?
Ambiguity is the rule of the corporate workplace. Companies move so fast, it's like a bus traveling 100 miles per hour and you're only going 80: You've got to get up to speed to find a seat on the bus if you truly want to be along for the ride.

Every day, good leaders fail. They're good people, smart people, kind people, and fun people, and yet they don't take their proper places at the top for one driving reason. What is it?

The real reason good leaders don't succeed isn't because they don't know what to do; they don't succeed because they don't make decisions about what to do. Success is about making all kinds of decisions, all day long.

This is, perhaps, the critical reason why an MBA isn't the guarantee of success it used to be: MBAs don't adequately prepare you for decision making in real time, in the real world, when it really counts. To succeed, you must make decisions. You won't always make the right decisions—that's not what success is about. But you must make enough of the right decisions enough of the time to move forward, to provide results, and to make up for those missing pieces of information that prevent many people from making a decision in the first place.

Fear, indecisiveness, ambiguity, hesitance, and procrastination are the real career killers. And it's not because most leaders are fearful, hesitant procrastinators—it's because they're waiting for the rest of the facts to come in before they decide something. But the rest of the facts will *never* come in. You've got to make some decisions based on instinct, on your gut, and on the facts you have in front of you.

You can't wait until you have all the facts in this day and age. Things move so quickly now that you have to be comfortable dealing with ambiguity and figuring out the rest on instinct.

Knowing the nine rules found in this book will help you get a seat on the bus.

Action Plan: Build Your Employment Pyramid

Earlier I discussed the importance of building your career from top to bottom using an employment pyramid. In your first action plan, build your pyramid from the ground up:

The Bottom of Your Employment Pyramid

Remember, everything you've done to date has value. However, in corporate America anyway, some things are simply more valuable than others.

For example, we all have certain biases. Maybe you're being interviewed by a corporate executive who doesn't have an MBA, who went to school on a sports scholarship and worked up to the top of the corporation the old-fashioned way. Now, this is not to say that this person will have a chip on his or her shoulder, but if you're an academics-only candidate who makes the MBA the top of your employment pyramid, you're not going to have much to talk about with this person.

So you need to have some backup skills, awards, achievements, recognitions, and so on to make sure you are a well-rounded and serious employee candidate. With that in mind, list the five to seven qualities, accomplishments, degrees, or awards you believe form the base, or bottom, of your employment pyramid:

_____

_____

_____

The Middle of Your Employment Pyramid

Now, let's add another layer to your attractiveness to employers. Building with the solid foundation you've laid at the bottom of your employment pyramid, stack three to four additional items you think give your résumé or interview another dimension:

_____

_____

_____

_____

The Top of Your Employment Pyramid

Now top this employment pyramid off by adding those two to three qualities, skills, achievements, habits, awards, or recognitions you've achieved that really make your résumé irresistible to employers:

_____

_____

_____

Finally, let's prioritize accordingly and put your pyramid right side up. Next to each location on the employment pyramid, list the quality or qualities that belong there, based on what you listed above:

- Top: _____
- Middle: _____
- Bottom: _____

Rule #2

The All-Inclusive Résumé—What Really Counts!

RULE #2 FOR HOW TO PLAY THE GAME AT THE TOP centers on what I call the all-inclusive résumé. What's the difference between a regular résumé and one that's all-inclusive? That's a little like asking, which one would you rather eat if you were really, really hungry: a hamburger or a double-super-duper-burger? Or which car would you rather drive: a midsize sedan or a luxury sedan?

Simply put, an all-inclusive résumé is analogous to the consummate executives that were discussed in Rule #1—book smart but also street smart, that is, smart enough to know the rules on the corporate website tell only half the story; bright enough to fill in the blanks—and read between the lines—for themselves.

In short, the whole package.

An all-inclusive résumé lists the essentials presented in a regular résumé: education, background, and experience. But then it goes one step further and lists what really counts. In this chapter, you'll understand what the recruiters, the HR professionals, the VPs, and the CEOs— the people who are looking at résumés—*really* want to know.

And what these hiring professionals really want to know, what separates an all-inclusive résumé from a regular résumé is something that's hard to put in writing. It's called the X-Factor.

Think of the X-Factor as the something that burns inside, that unquenchable desire that stays lit through good times and bad, that drive that found you seeking this career and picking up this book in the first place.

The X-Factor is your commitment to the job, the choices you seek out, the extracurricular activities you engage in, and your real motivation for wanting—and getting—the job.

It all starts with honesty.

Be Honest: Emphasize Ethics and Values

As recent scandals show, including Bernie Madoff and the disgraced executives at Enron, ethics and values haven't exactly been top priorities for corporate leaders in recent years. That trend is rapidly changing.

For a time, corporate America was all about profits, bottom-line margins, and return on investment. That's capitalism, to be sure, but how much is too much? In raking up huge numbers, we often forgot about who, exactly, was making those profits, margins, and ROIs possible in the first place—the frontline employees and support staff who worked at those companies, often far away from those in the corner offices and their seven-figure bonuses.

When Enron went down, thousands of hardworking, innocent, and loyal employees lost not only their livelihoods but their life savings; many also lost faith in the executives of corporate America. They weren't alone. America in general has become fed up with corporate greed, loose ethics, and diminished values. Why should corporate America care? For one thing, when Americans get hold of an idea, they can vote with their dollars. Likewise, when they're fed up with someone, they can vote someone out. Social networking and the Internet have made word of mouth lightning fast and increasingly relevant.

Have a bad customer service experience with your credit card company? In minutes the whole world can know about it. Have a bad meal at a big chain restaurant? A couple of tweets later, thousands of people in your social network can know every minor detail of the experience. And if Americans choose to boycott a company, the lightning-fast immediacy of Facebook, Twitter, and a million individual blogs make it easier than ever for word to spread.

To bring companies back into balance, leaders of the future need to be more aware of ethics and how one's ethical DNA affects one's future position within the organization. Even if you're just starting out and are nowhere near making executive decisions that affect the social responsibility of your company, know that every voice counts. Not only that, but everyone is looking.

The decisions you make on a daily basis, how you respond to moral dilemmas even at the entry level, can be projected into the future and can tell your supervisors and their supervisors how you might deal with bigger issues higher up in the company. It's never too early to start making executive decisions, even at the entry level. No one in the organization is exempt from corporate responsibility.

Yes, this means *you*. Yes, you have an obligation as a future game player to think of the employees who you might one day lead. In the past 10 years, people in senior leadership have made decisions for themselves versus the shareholders or employees. These self-serving decisions have often been the source of reduced profits, tarnished reputations, bankruptcies, and, in some cases, even the downfall of the entire company.

Now it is your turn to start making decisions that affect not only you, but shareholders and employees as well. As a new corporate employee, it is a modern reality that while you are an individual, at heart you are also a team player, a part of the process, and a member of something larger than yourself.

We all must make self-serving decisions every day—that is human nature. However, we must also work as a team to make responsible decisions that affect the company for which we work.

In later chapters, this book will discuss what your employers really want—one of those things is results. Results come when individuals working together as a team make decisions that positively reflect the company. At the heart of those decisions is honesty.

Why Honesty Matters

People who work in HR are highly trained individuals who are especially qualified to make hiring decisions; that's why they are where they are, doing what they do. When they're hiring people who could potentially be playing at the top, they take their jobs very, very seriously.

One of the biggest things HR representatives look for in a résumé and during an interview is honesty. Now, why should it matter if one lowly entry-level employee fudges his résumé a bit? What if one prospective candidate says she has a graduate degree when, really, she only has a bachelor's degree? No doubt you have seen some of the biggest names in corporate America dragged through the mud in recent years because of scandals that involved dishonesty, fraud, and less-than-stellar ethics.

One's ethics now are a great future indicator of one's ethics later. So if at the entry level you're already playing fast and loose with the truth, how much faster and looser will your truth-dealing be when you've been on the job for a few years and know exactly what you can and can't get away with? Good HR reps know that the person who lies early will lie even more later on, so they are on high alert for spotting the truth—and detecting deception.

What interviewers really want to know is this: Did you really do all the things you say you did on your résumé? Many people have been caught in lies around what they did and what they didn't do.

While these lies may seem harmless at the time, they are not viewed in a vacuum. Instead, they are viewed in relation to what lying about this particular instance says about your character. In other words, if you would lie about your degree, former position, or marital status on something like a résumé, what else would you lie about?

Never forget that someday, as an executive, you will be representing your company to the highest level of ethical responsibility available. How can you be trusted to represent the company truthfully if you can't represent yourself truthfully?

It's important that you're honest at all times, but particularly when you put something in writing. (After all, nowadays writing is forever.) It's important that you actually did all those things that you put on your résumé. So if you say you have your MBA, have it. If you say you were in the senior drama program, I hope you really did that.

Now more than ever, with high school records, yearbooks, and even grades easily accessed or checked electronically, the HR department can quickly determine what's true or not true on your résumé; nothing kills a career like an inaccurate or even falsified résumé.

The Dangers of Social Networking

Recently I ran across an article that talked about a woman who was fired because of what she wrote on her Facebook page. Apparently she had called in sick a few times one month and her boss, getting suspicious, started digging around online.

What the boss discovered was that the employee in question had posted pictures from various parties, and tracking backward with a calendar in hand, he noted that the parties always occurred on the night before this employee called in sick.

The employee said to the reporter, more or less, "What I do on my own time is my business. I had no right to be fired."

And when asked about that quote, the boss noted that, absolutely, she has the right to her private life—so long as it doesn't interfere with her work.

What I realized while reading that article was that we are raising an entire generation to believe it is their right, their duty, almost their responsibility to post almost every moment of their lives online. It is nothing for today's younger generation to snap photos of their most intimate, boring, revealing, important, and mundane moments and post them for all the world to see. Again, this is absolutely within your rights as a private citizen of this very free country.

However, know in advance that your bosses; your HR department; and your coworkers, colleagues, managers, and supervisors have the same online access that you have. If you are going to enjoy a rich and robust private life—and especially if you are going to post pictures of it, blog about it, publish it online, or share it with friends through the latest social network—know that it could get you in trouble.

I've seen several employees get into hot water over things they wrote—or simply reposted—online about their job, their responsibilities, their boss, his boss, her boss, and on up the line. Where does your private life end and your professional life begin? I would hope I don't have to tell you, but if you have to ask, you probably already suspect that you're crossing it!

In short, when posting anything online—pictures, blogs, opinions, rants, raves, reviews, and so on—ask yourself this one simple question, "Would I be comfortable if my boss read this?"

If so, go for it.

If not, think twice.

Again, this section is not designed to censor you in any way but only to remind you that companies are not democracies; you won't get a chance to bring the issue to vote. If your boss decides that what you've posted online about yourself, the company, the company's products or services, and/or your boss is a fireable offense, well, it probably was. And even if it wasn't, the lines are so fuzzy that it will be hard to prove your case.

Why take the chance?

Unfortunately, this goes for new hires as well. Even if you aren't working for the company yet, even if what you posted online was two years old, even if what you wrote about your last company—or the last bachelor party you attended—was done in haste and in the heat of the moment, there it is online for all the world, including any hiring committee that wants to Google you, to see. (Believe me, they *all* use Google these days.)

So watch what you post online, especially if you're considering becoming a consummate executive one day. The new reality is that while you are free to post whatever you want online these days, the alternate view is that future and current employees are just as free to find it, consider it, and, ultimately, use it to reward or punish you. Fair or not, such is capitalism and the world of corporate America.

Intestinal Fortitude: Do You Have It?

I started this book off with a simple quote: "The will to win is the will to prepare to win." This is not a quote about winning, per se, or touchdowns or home runs or millions or even billions of dollars.

It is, in fact, a quote about something I like to call "intestinal fortitude." In other words, do you have the stomach to win? Can you handle the stress when things heat up and all doesn't go your way? Do you have what it takes to make the tough decisions, to face your fears, and to take the steps you'll need to prepare to win?

Job candidates often approach the interview process by rote and treat their résumés with equal formality. But while every résumé should follow a certain pattern and meet the basic criteria that modern companies currently require, interviewers are also looking for intestinal fortitude.

Intestinal fortitude can also be described as that inner fire, that burning inside that says you're hungry for success, eager to meet new challenges, willing to take a risk, and dogged in your determination to win and provide benefits for the company. It can also be called your X-Factor—or what goes into a résumé, a career, or a life that can't be covered in 25 words or less.

In other words, what can future employees read between the lines about you that sets you apart from the rest? It's hard to describe what HR departments are looking for when it comes to the X-Factor other than "they'll know it when they see it."

You can just tell when someone has intestinal fortitude—the X-Factor—when he or she walks into the room. It's on the résumé, yes, but it's also in so many other things that person does and says during the interview: how he dresses, how she carries herself, whether he looks you in the eye, if she answers quickly and firmly, how he phrases his responses, and so on.

Beyond the Résumé: Writing—and Reading—Between the Lines

In addition to what you've typed up, printed, and brought along with you in the black and white of your résumé, HR departments are also looking for things *beyond the résumé*; such as personal interests, accomplishments, or skills that reveal your inner desire not just for wanting this specific job with this specific company but also a long-term career as a consummate executive in this field.

The individuals who make hiring decisions are looking for information that will reveal what's really driving you and how committed you are to learning quickly and producing results consistently. What's the burning desire you have inside of you that really makes me, as the interviewer, believe that you're the right person for the job?

Remember that people, not robots, make hiring decisions. Yes, you must have a stellar résumé that knocks their socks off, but you can't just drop it off wearing a Hawaiian shirt and flip-flops! Much like your MBA or any other award, skill, or recognition you bring with you to the interview, your résumé is but a mere facet of who you present to the HR staff.

To say you have a degree in public speaking is all but useless if you mumble during your interview, never make eye contact, and can't form a complete sentence! To succeed in today's competitive climate, you have to be able to articulate those skills, those desires, those personality traits, beyond your black-and-white experiences as printed on your résumé.

You have to go beyond just saying, "Oh, I have an MBA," "Oh, I had a 4.0 GPA," or "Oh, by the way, I was class valedictorian." These are marvelous accomplishments and absolutely have merit. They belong on your résumé in bold print and will, in fact, make a difference come hiring time. But how much of a difference they make depends on how well you have displayed what you've done with that MBA and GPA and what being a class valedictorian taught you.

Success is not just about who has the biggest toolbox but what each person does with his or her own set of tools. I've seen many consummate executives succeed without the usual pedigree of an Ivy League education and their parents' high-worth connections, and I've seen just as many would-be executives fail despite their MBA, their 4.0 GPA, and their status as class valedictorian.

I've sat in on the hiring process of many would-be executives and know this part of the interview process intimately. What I can tell you is that in interview after interview, HR reps see the same résumés, the same qualifications, and the same attributes in candidate after candidate.

To think you're going to walk into an interview at a *Fortune* 500 company and blow the interviewers away based on your résumé alone isn't just naive, it's harmful to your potentially getting the job. You must realize how many résumés these hiring professionals read and how important it is to complement your résumé with items that make you stand out as not just a human being but also as the right candidate for the job.

These days, so many other candidates also have these same qualities that interviewers need to know more—and so many candidates who don't have these qualities do more to prove themselves, personally and creatively, that merely checking off the MBA, GPA, or class valedictorian slots on your résumé are no longer enough.

Interviewers want to get to know you personally. They want to see what traits you have, what qualities you possess, that will set you apart from the other interviewees and send you straight to the top. And they know what to look for. One thing they look for is that burning inside, that X-Factor, that says, "Pick me. I'm the one!"

What Is Your Modus Operandi (M.O.)?

When individual candidates are being interviewed, the HR staff is assessing what they are all about. It goes beyond what's on paper to the person who, at that moment, is sitting in front of the interviewer. How is he or she wired, meaning, what is driving him or her? What's motivating him or her? What impels commitment, the will to succeed, and the drive to work harder? What would be *your* commitment to achieving success? What will be your commitment to this company that is looking to hire you?

Is the commitment just showing up from 9 a.m. to 5 p.m.? Is it working until quitting time, or is it going beyond the call of duty to work overtime, do extra duties, learn more, and supplement on-the-job training with extra classes, seminars, and workshops?

All this means is that sometimes you come in early. Sometimes you stay late. Sometimes you take a phone call from another country in the evening because you know that if there's a meeting going on at 8 a.m. in Asia, well, that's nighttime for your counterparts in America, so you suck it up and schedule accordingly.

This idea reflects those unwritten rules of corporate America I spoke of earlier. Nowhere in your job description does it say, "Stay past 5 p.m., take the call, and make the client happy." However, we all know that to succeed, we have to go beyond what it says in print in our employee handbook. If your client in Asia can't speak at any time other than 8 a.m. in his or her country and that means 8 p.m.

where you live, what are you going to do? Skip the call? Pass the buck to someone else? What does that mean for the person you pass the buck to? *That person* has to stay late?

Lots of employees have families, and everyone has responsibilities and needs free time—I'm not telling you to sacrifice friends, family, health, or free time to become a workaholic. Too often in my career I've seen peers and employees have a lack of balance in their work life. It's imperative that you keep proper perspective on what really matters. You can always find another job, but you only have one time to capture those special moments with your kids and loved ones like I have with my two boys, Fenorris Jr. and Nicholas, who are developing into two fine young men. That said, duty does occasionally call, and, on those occasions, you have one of two choices: answer the call or ignore it.

I think it's safe to say that your supervisor is going to reward those who answer the call of duty and, if not outright punish, then at least withhold all or some reward from those who ignore the call. And if you do take the call at 8 p.m. on one night, it doesn't mean you have to do so every night; with flexible schedules, you can benefit accordingly by coming in later the next morning or making up the time elsewhere. The important thing is that you're working smart—that is, doing what you need to do without killing yourself to do it—as opposed to working hard.

Which Reality Is Yours?

In life, there are two realities:

1. How you'd like things to be
2. The way things really are

We'd all like to work 40 hours a week and enjoy leisurely weekends at home with the ones we love, and quite often that happens. However, the way things really are is that sometimes you work 80 hours for six weeks straight; sometimes you eat lunch at your desk, spend all day locked in a conference room with the finance committee, and have to get into town early to meet a foreign client. So for consummate executives, the only reality that matters is what's behind door # 2: the way things really are.

Are you willing to go beyond the call of duty, or are you the type of employee who is just coming in to work 9 a.m. to 5 p.m.? Are you going to stubbornly stick to your own personal reality and stick your head in the sand, no matter what's going on around you, or are you going to respond to the way things really are? That's an example of your commitment to the job. Beyond your résumé, beyond your experiences, what's motivating you to apply for this job?

Now, how do you put all of this information on a résumé? How do you explain your passion, your commitment, your burning desire, and your X-Factor on a single sheet of paper? It's actually easier than it sounds because a winner is easy to spot. That's why it's so important to learn these nine rules now, because the sooner you accept these things and make them your new reality, the faster they become part of your personality.

You can't fake success; it either is or it isn't. Likewise, modern interviewers know the difference between someone with potential for true success or someone who just looks good on paper. And beyond the résumé, what really matters to hiring personnel is your potential for success. That starts with your dreams, your burning desire—your X-Factor.

As the interviewer, I'm trained to see if a person's motivation is just money or just a desire to say "I work for this company." In other words, are you only in it for the dollars or the prestige of working for Company X, and are not really here to give me—and the company— what we're going to need from you?

So I have to ask myself the following questions that go beyond what you've put on your résumé and what you've worn to this interview:

- What's really motivating you?
- What is your M.O.?
- In other words, what is motivating you to get this job?

You have to make sure, as you're sitting across the table and you're applying for a job, that the interviewer knows, beyond your résumé, that you have an intense desire to help the company win.

The interviewer needs to understand that you're not just out for yourself, that you're more than a team player—that you're consummate executive material. And how you relate those qualities is through a passionate commitment to excellence. And when you have that commitment, it shows up in and beyond the résumé.

Beyond the degrees and accomplishments, you must speak to how, specifically, you can help the company win. That is always the most important quality *any* candidate possesses.

You may be applying at the most altruistic company on the planet, but the people interviewing you are not here to donate to charity; they are there to hire the best person for the job. And the person who helps the company win—now and in the future—is the one who gets the job.

Helping the company succeed should be your ultimate motivation to work for any company, because in today's globally competitive environment, companies are trying to win now more than ever. And they want the people joining that company to be serious about helping them win and ethically doing all the things that are necessary to win.

Right now it's about getting the job, but even in your zeal to get the job, you must keep the company's focus of the company ever in your mind. In America, we are taught "me first." In corporate America, we must learn "company first."

Right or wrong, fair or unfair, if you want to succeed in corporate America, if you want to play at the top, if you want to be a consummate executive, you have to respect the company and recognize that it comes first. So don't approach the interview, or even the résumé, with a "me first" attitude. Consider the interview with the "company first" perspective.

So haul out your current résumé and read it with a fresh perspective. Does it sound like a brag list, or do the qualities you possess, the achievements you've had, the awards you've won, and the affiliations you have speak to becoming an effective member of the company? If so, you have an all-inclusive résumé; if not, go back to the drawing board!

Lessons from the Gridiron

The other factors the hiring team is considering center on extracurricular activities. Extracurricular activities include things like working in your community, playing in a band, joining clubs, donating your time, and of course, playing sports. One of the things that helped me as I explored opportunities within other corporations was playing sports; this was, in fact, a huge asset for me.

I wasn't the class valedictorian, but I was a pretty good student. At the end of the day, however, what helped me achieve significantly in school was playing sports.

Sports allowed me the ability to hone in on my leadership skills, because, when you look at sports today, you find a lot of professional coaches who are asked to come into corporate America to speak about leadership.

Why is that? Well there are actually some very specific reasons why coaches, or even former athletes, make great leaders:

- *Working with people from different types of backgrounds.* When you're a college athlete, you are playing with people from all over the world. Even when you go to a state college, you're not just interacting with kids from Florida or Georgia or California or Michigan. Nowadays, most colleges recruit both domestically and internationally. So now you get the chance to work with all different kinds of personalities, all different types of skill sets. This experience helped me manage people from different countries and backgrounds; in the global economy, this skill is vitally important. In particular, I wound up heading a global department for Dell and, having worked with international students in sports, I felt prepared to begin what would have otherwise been a very challenging assignment for me.

- *Leadership skills.* I happened to be the captain of my team. We had a lot of success, playing in NCAA basketball tournaments, and we even won a couple of championships within our conference, so that allowed me to learn how to lead, how to talk to people, and how to motivate people and get the best from them. If you can lead a team—whether it's a sports team, an academic team, a military team, and so on—you come to corporate America knowing how to turn groups of people into effective teams. That's one quality most companies would fight for.

- *Managing time.* Time management is critical in today's corporate environment. You have to learn how to manage your time. Especially today, employees are charged with doing more work with fewer resources, time being the most precious resource of all! So when you're a student athlete, you have all the other time constraints of a student *plus* a nearly full-time sports regimen. With obligations to practice, classes, team meetings, extracurricular activities, clubs, games, traveling for games, and other activities, if you can't manage your time as a student athlete, you'll end up being neither a student nor an athlete.

- *Discipline.* You had to go to class, and you had to go to practice. You had to be on time and perform at the top of your game, and you couldn't do one without the other. Let your grades suffer, and you're off the team. Let your practice suffer, and you're *still* off the team! And so all of those skill sets translate and transition into being a successful part of corporate America.

- *Managing people.* You have to learn how to motivate people. What's more, you can't motivate everyone in quite the same way because people respond differently. While one or two people on your team may respond to logic, three others won't. What *will* those people respond to? You have to find out. For instance, some teammates will respond to the emotional aspect of winning the game ("Let's win this one for the Gipper!"), while others are more logical ("One more touchdown and we're in the finals!"). Learning how to motivate people in sports, in a club, on a team, and so on, helps prepare you for this mission-critical job skill.

- *Learn how to deal with overcoming defeat.* Hollywood has happy endings where everyone succeeds because of hard work, integrity, and just plain stick-to-itiveness. In corporate America, you're going to lose some battles, and if you don't know how to deal with that you're going to crumble long before you ever have a chance to shine. Losing on the field helped me prepare for losses in the boardroom, but the elements that went into my education and background helped me overcome these to succeed many times over despite the occasional loss.

Of course, these skills—time and people management, multitasking, leadership, working with different groups of people—are found in many extracurricular activities, so don't be discouraged if sports wasn't, and still isn't, your thing.

If your extracurricular activity was drama, for instance, you learn to manage your time and work with many different types of people. You learn to lead a group and motivate an audience. As a cheerleader or pep squad or flag corps member, you have to lead and be disciplined. If your extracurricular activities are related to church, skills in leadership, organization, and time and people management can be found there as well.

Having extracurricular activities on your résumé matters, and people on the hiring committee do consider such information to determine the strength of your X-Factor. Whether you're playing sports or participating in the Spanish club or chess club, all of your extracurricular activities matter to the right person at the right time. They are a part of the equation someone is using to assess you as a potential part of the organization.

Umm... So What Else Are You Doing?

Many people think life stops after graduation; those people aren't likely to become consummate executives anytime soon. And I don't say that to be harsh, but true consummate executives—even those in training—know that success never stands still.

If you graduate in May and your first major interview isn't until August, fine: enjoy yourself but don't ever, ever, *ever* stop learning and filling your résumé with X-Factor material. Consummate executives are always moving, always shaking, always learning, and always doing one more thing to add to their value to the organization. If that means taking a class here or subscribing to a magazine there, so be it. If that means taking up golf because the clients love it, all the better.

In short, never let an opportunity pass you by. If you want to play at the top of the top companies in this country, you'll need to know when it's time to relax, stay the course, increase your speed, or downright put the pedal to the metal. So if you graduate and have two or three months before "real life" begins, by all means, enjoy yourself for a few weeks but then get it in gear and keep moving forward.

Join a club for like-minded graduates. Learn all you can about a company by following its stock price and reading its website. Take a summer class. Do anything to keep the gears running smoothly and your mind active and current.

I mentioned earlier some of the extracurricular activities that you could partake in while you're in school. But what do you need to do *after* you have finished school to continue not just learning but also building your all-inclusive résumé?

Various important extracurricular activities are essential for you to be a part of as you work toward a secure position in corporate America. And by important, I mean the opposite of fluff. Anyone can take basket weaving, join a gym, or start a club, but the question to ask yourself before doing so is: Will this be seen as helping the company in some way?

So if you join a club, make it Future Business Leaders of America or Phi Beta Lambda, not Hardcore Joystick Gamers and Slackers Unite! If you are going to take a class in basket weaving to further your career, make sure it's because the division you want to run at Company XYZ makes baskets! If you're going to read a magazine, it can help your career if you do so in the attempt to write an article and get it published with your byline so you can be known as an expert on this particular subject. In other words, spare time is fine, but don't just spin your wheels—use that time wisely. You might also try to be a part of professional organizations that are within your field of expertise.

You have to remember that hiring staff is going to be looking at putting like with like: apples with apples and oranges with oranges. In other words, did you engage in extracurricular activities that guided you closer to your ultimate destination, be it sales or PR or organizational development or R & D, or did you just do basket weaving to stay busy?

So, if you have a marketing degree, you probably should find professional organizations that are affiliated with marketing. Maybe you could intern in the creative department of a local advertising agency or take a course in jingle writing from an accredited online university. If you have a management degree, then you would probably want to find professional organizations that are focused on management, leadership, and other related concerns.

And don't stop there. If an appropriate group doesn't exist in your area, start one. Find local young people or recent management graduates and work together to learn more, do more, share more, and connect more on the subject that really matters to you most. Meet regularly and give your group a name so that you can list it on your résumé.

It's important to try to show that you have the capacity to do other things beyond your degree that are both in your field and in the field of people. In other words, yes you need to skills to do the job but you will also need those very critical people skills to get others to help you do the job. No position exists in a vacuum; we are all part of teams, even the vaulted "leadership" and "management" teams.

Many recent graduates with MBAs have very little proven management or leadership skills and so joining these extracurricular organizations after graduating will not only help you acquire the people skills you'll need to succeed at the top of the game but will also demonstrably prove to the all-important hiring board that you have such skills.

Participating in events associated with some type of professional organization really helps the interviewer conclude that a candidate has the capacity to multitask in the proper areas according to his or her expertise.

What's more, it also helps the interviewer understand that you're constantly trying to better yourself, constantly trying to surround yourself with people who are striving to be the best they can be, and learning from each other. That's very helpful information to someone who's looking to hire you, and all of it belongs on the all-inclusive résumé.

"Like with like" applies to people, too. You have to realize that in business, people want to work with people who are like them. That doesn't mean they want to work with people who look just like them. Hard work is the universal language of success. People who work hard tend to surround themselves with people who work hard. Having lots of extracurricular activities shows people that you work hard.

People who work in HR departments—interviewers, staffers, researchers, organizers, and assistants—work hard, too. So when you're being interviewed and someone who works hard spots a fellow hard worker, the interviewer's "like with like" meter goes off and that person thinks more highly of you. It's only natural. So don't skimp on the extracurricular activities if your goal is to play at the top.

Beyond the Résumé—Measuring What Really Counts

Education is critical for success, but if every candidate has the same education from the same Ivy League schools and the same GPA, how can you stand out? Other factors beyond education—business etiquette, dress, playing well with others, dedication to the team, extracurricular activities, poise, and grace—are easy to measure and log. But what of those immeasurable traits—passion, drive, commitment, and stamina—that count just as much in the corner office?

The immeasurable is really the decision behind the decision. Interviewers are faced with what they can see—your nice business suit, your professional haircut, your smile, your résumé—and what they can't see, such as your desire, commitment, sincerity, and so on.

Don't make the mistake of thinking that the external, what interviewers can see, is all that counts. Yes, the surface things matter, but they are not all that matters. In fact, when it comes to success, it is often the unseen that matters the most.

Think about it: all candidates come to the interview dressed up, looking their best, prepared to be grilled, and holding a freshly printed résumé that shows them in their best light. So in this assembly-line process of interviewing one well-qualified applicant after another, the interviewer must often make a final determination based on a candidate's unseen qualities.

When it comes to playing at the top, it's often the intense, burning desire of the candidate—his or her internally felt and externally evidenced X-Factor—that makes the final decision. So if you did not go to an Ivy League school, don't let that fact hold you back from playing at the top of the game.

Work hard at your job, do what you're supposed to do, and do it better than anybody else. Learn constantly, listen attentively, and show that you're learning and listening. Remember, results matter: they are the external evidence of your internal X-Factor. Performance and results are two of the most important traits a top performer can possess. The third trait can't be measured with grades or paychecks or promotions or time cards or, for that matter, a résumé: that trait is what's inside your heart.

Never underestimate yourself or let someone tell you that you can't get to the top. Dreams are crushed by negativity, not reality. If you hear you're worthless, not smart enough, don't have the right pedigree, unqualified, or "not the right material" long enough, you tend to believe it. It's true, unfortunately, that plenty of people will try to impede your trip to the top. Don't let them.

Believe in yourself but, more importantly, prove yourself.

Don't play the victim if you got your MBA from a state university or didn't letter in varsity sports. Treat every job you've got like you're doing it from the corner office, and I guarantee you that, after a few such performances, no one will even remember where you went to school—or that you didn't play sports!

This is the driving force behind success: it's not who you know or where you went to school or what sport you played or what sex or color you are or the car you drive that determines success. It's what you do that counts.

Performance is all; perform well and it won't matter that the high school equivalency is the highest degree you've earned. Perform poorly and your Harvard or Yale education won't keep you from getting the axe.

If you're insecure about your educational or social pedigree, performance will erase that insecurity with every feat, skill, success, or accomplishment. If you're prideful, boastful, or too reliant on your educational or social pedigree, with every failure, you will feel and act less secure.

There are measurable skills and immeasurable skills that determine one's success in corporate America today:

- Measurable: school, grades, testimonials, work records, past performance, and so on
- Immeasurable: heart, desire, goals, stamina, passion, willingness to succeed, and so on

Top performers—and those who hire them—are as concerned about the traits they can measure as they are about the immeasurable ones. When I'm selecting someone for my team or my department—or, for that matter, my replacement—I always look closely at the measurable skills, but I also work hard to decipher those immeasurable skills the candidates possess as well.

How can I tell?

- When someone is hungry, you can sense it.
- When someone has a burning desire to succeed, you can feel it.
- And when someone is destined for the top, you can actually see it.

Why do I look so hard beyond the résumé, the GPA, the dress code, and the hair gel? Because so many of the top performers in my company, and in corporate America in general, defy conventions to go completely off the charts and create a new breed of success altogether.

That's what I'm looking for, because that's what top performers are made of.

Action Plan for the All-Inclusive Résumé: Rewrite the Mission Statement

If I had a dime for every generic mission statement I read at the beginning of every résumé that sounded something like "To use my mission-critical skills to further evidence the vision of my success by intertwining my own goals with those of the corporate creed through determination, focus, and charisma to change the corporate paradigm of success," I would be printing this book on gold leaf and giving it away by the pallet!

Remember that it's an assembly line out there on the job front, and the surest way to get your résumé ignored is by making it look just like everybody else's! So in this action plan, focus not on writing a cookie-cutter mission statement just to sound good, but to really reveal your personality and make it actually mean something.

While a printable sample of the all-inclusive résumé can be found on my website at www.corporateclimb.net, for now let's get active about rewriting your mission statement in the here and now.

Much has been written about this critical item, but what I want to read in a mission statement has two critical parts:

- *Part 1:* What makes *you* so special?
- *Part 2:* What can *you* do for *me*?

Notice that this new mission statement has to do with you and me, not just some generic, cookie-cutter message that has no relevance to either of us.

Notice also that this mission statement has two parts; if you make each part a complete thought and include it in one sentence, you will have what I call the all-inclusive mission statement.

Following are several spaces for you to practice your mission statement, with a final place for a "clean" version that should speak to both of the necessary parts.

Rough Draft(s) of Your Mission Statement(s)

_____

_____

_____

_____

Final Draft of Your Mission Statement

_____

_____

_____

_____

Rule #3

Get Sponsored to Change Your Career Overnight

WHAT IF THERE WERE ONE PERSON OUT THERE who could take your career to that next level? What if that person could take your career not just to the next level but to the very top of the game? This is not a mentor or mere colleague, but a high-level alpha player who, with one bold decision, could completely change your game—and your life—and put you on a completely new trajectory toward untold wealth, accomplishment, and success.

The good news is that such a person exists. The even better news is that despite the layoffs, the economy, the downsizing, the foreclosures, and the bleak, terrible, gut-wrenching financial forecast, such people are more necessary than ever.

Who is this person, and how can you find him or her?

A sponsor is that one individual who can make all the difference. I'm not just talking about your boss or your boss's boss, or even the CEO. A sponsor can be anyone, anywhere, who takes a personal interest in you and decides to give you that leg up you deserve.

Say you work for a nonprofit organization and you meet someone at the Ford Foundation who, with one simple phone call, can get you a $5 million grant that saves the day, makes your career, and establishes your credentials instantly. That's a sponsor.

Maybe you're a new hire at a *Fortune* 500 company and no one in the accounting department there appreciates your self-starting, entrepreneurial, get-up-and-go attitude. So you go on the offensive and join a Ladies Who Lunch panel that meets three times a week. There you are introduced to a well-dressed woman who just happens to be on the lookout for a self-starting, entrepreneurial, get-up-and-go head of accounting at her company. Meet your new sponsor!

Perhaps you're teaching tennis part-time at the country club while you take night classes to earn your MBA. That middle-aged guy who's a little puffy around the middle but runs the biggest chain of gyms in the regional Southeast isn't just your best client—by getting him to hire you to manage his new personal training company, he just became your sponsor.

How is sponsorship different from mere networking? Networking is casting a wide net and hoping to reel in a fresh haul of a dozen or more hopefully helping hands. Finding a sponsor is a more active, singular pursuit; you are specifically looking for that one person to change your whole game and take you straight to the top. And in this day and age, you're going to need a sponsor sooner than later.

Sponsor Your Way to the Top

These days, competition isn't just stiff; it's survival of the fittest! Now more than ever, you need every advantage you've got, particularly if you're a recent grad, internal employee of a company or an institution, a woman, or a minority.

And it's not just in corporate America where all the competitive slack is being taken up. Like a ripple effect, nonprofit organizations, educational institutions, the entrepreneurial world, and smaller businesses are becoming increasingly competitive, making the need more imperative for sponsors in almost every nook, cranny, and niche.

Think hard work, an MBA, and a well-rounded résumé will get you to the top? Think a plucky attitude and a three-piece suit will get you noticed, promoted, elected, funded, or rewarded? Think again. That might be what got you here, but to get to the top, you'll need more than just a spotless résumé, a 4.0 GPA, outstanding results, a #1 spot on the succession planning chart, and a reputation as being the top performer in your business unit. You'll need a sponsor.

Get Sponsored!

That's the next rule you need to play the game at the top. And believe me, this single rule has the power to change your career overnight. That is what sponsorship means: meeting the person who can literally take you from entry level to the top of your game simply by showing an interest in your career.

But to get to that point, you need to understand a few basics about sponsorship. So in this chapter, I will explain what a sponsor is, what it takes to get sponsored, what role a sponsor plays, how I got sponsored, and how one goes about getting a sponsor.

The Difference between a Mentor and a Sponsor

Some people misconstrue mentorship with sponsorship. A mentor is a person who is willing to take some time to coach you on how to dress for success, how to talk for success, and even how to prepare for success. A mentor is someone who can help you think through some of the challenges that you're having at work—someone who could coach you on how to deal with a cohort or similar issues.

A mentor is a guide, an adviser, a tutor, even a guru. And you would usually meet with that mentor once every quarter, once every month, depending on the relationship you have with the mentor.

Mentors give guidance, lead by example, and provide wisdom to help you on your path to success. Their roles are vital, but only through the means of support. They do not actively intercede on your behalf or physically act to improve your position or foster your success.

Mentors' professional and even financial futures are not invested in yours; there's no tie-in for them to act on your behalf. Like the best teachers, parents, friends, and role models, mentors help guide you to success rather than becoming the actual facilitator of that success.

Sponsors may consult and advise in addition to their more active role, but they also clear the path for promotions, or more challenging and demanding projects, and they may even take you with them if they leave the present company or start a new business venture of their own.

A mentor is great—a super adviser, a great resource when you need a guru or other career advice—but a sponsor takes a much more active role in your success than a mentor.

Sponsorship Defined

Sponsors are all about action; they actively facilitate your success through their sponsorship. In the most literal sense, you become their protégé—someone guided and protected by a more prominent individual at your company.

A mentor is not a sponsor, and a sponsor is not a mentor. A sponsor will say, "You're someone who I have a vested interest in from a success perspective," or, in other words, "I'm willing to put all my professional and corporate political capital on the line to ensure that you achieve the success you want to achieve." Mentors are wonderful— they can really help you be in a position to get considered for the job. But understand that a sponsor brings closure to the situation and is more definitive in his or her role.

A mentor will say, "Let me help you prepare for your job or new responsibilities. You go and talk to this person. You go and talk to that person. These people will help you. Then come back to me and we'll reconvene and see about preparing you for this job." But a sponsor wouldn't tell you to go here or go there. A sponsor would say, unequivocally, "That is your job. No ifs, ands, or buts about it. That is your job."

What's the difference? If you're interviewing for a job, and you have a mentor, the mentor is providing you with insights on how to prepare for the job. He or she is not a sponsor, because the mentor can't provide you with the exact details of that job. As you prepare for the interview for the job, a sponsor would be able to tell you, "That's your job."

Now, Go Get a Sponsor

How do you get a sponsor? There's no silver-bullet answer. However, understand that there are some things that you can do to put yourself in a better position to get a sponsor.

One of the first things you need to be aware of is how to find common ground with senior executives. Get to know your board members and their interests and hobbies, what clubs they belong to, what they talk about in the halls, and who they befriend outside of the corner office. Then find some common ground. Maybe you both enjoy sports. Maybe every day after lunch, you see the executive coming back from the corporate gym lugging his tennis bag or a racquetball racquet. If this is one of your hobbies, it could be a great way to make an introduction—and find a sponsor.

Perhaps one of the corporate VPs is involved in the local community center drama department, or writes a great blog, or volunteers with children, or kayaks at your favorite park. What is it that you have in common, or could have in common, that will put you in touch with a potential sponsor in or out of the office?

Sometimes your sponsor finds you. In fact, I've been fortunate enough to have that situation happen to me. Likewise, I've had situations where I've asked a person to be my sponsor. But understand that in corporate America, when you transition a relationship from a mentorship to a sponsorship, there are pros and cons.

What you're trying to do here is not just to suck up to a potential sponsor but, in fact, to find one who shares your interests. So I'm not necessarily telling you to go out and learn kayaking to attract a sponsor, but if you do find your interests aligning with a VP or other C-level executive, pursue that connection. Maybe you go to the same church; maybe you find out he or she is going on a weekend retreat. This is a great opportunity to interact one-on-one in a familiar setting that is comfortable to you both.

Remember, sponsorship at all costs is not the goal. You do not want to align yourself with someone who doesn't share your same values, your same ethics, and your same code or canon of how you live your life. When I sought out a sponsor, I really wanted to understand what was this person's values were. I wasn't after success by all means necessary. I wasn't willing to align myself with someone who didn't necessarily match with my values. By getting to know a potential sponsor, by actively finding a way to spend more time with him or her, you want to understand more about the person's values. Are this person's beliefs in alignment with yours as they relate to how he or she treats people?

Do you want to associate yourself with a leader who hasn't necessarily had a lot of success with how he or she treats people, from a leadership perspective? Do you want to align yourself with a dictator, despot, or tyrant? You have to ask these hard questions because when an executive sponsors you, you take on that person's professional and emotional baggage, for better or worse. So that's one of the criteria you want to assess.

Sponsorship is a two-way street. You don't want to align yourself with someone who can tarnish your reputation, because you worked hard to put yourself in the position to be received and have someone to select you as a sponsor.

Another sponsorship criterion is considered from the sponsor's perspective: Are you someone who can help the sponsor? Do not misconstrue that question. You may have a lot of wonderful qualities, but that is not exactly why the sponsor is selecting you. Maybe you are nice and the sponsor is nice and wants to work with nice people; that may be a part of the equation. But every equation has a sum, and that sum is the bottom line of what a sponsor gets out of the relationship. Understand that the sponsor's first criterion is, "Can he or she help me achieve success?"

In other words, "Can he or she help me *win*...?"

If you haven't put yourself in the position where you have done things to show symbolically that you can help a potential sponsor, then you're probably going to have less of a chance of getting sponsored.

Five Ways to Look Good to a Sponsor

It's important when looking for a sponsor that you make it worth that person's while to sponsor you. It's very rare to find a person in corporate America who is just looking to give someone the career boost he or she needs without getting anything in return. So be ready to give as good as you get. Be ready to use the following five ways to look good to a sponsor:

1. *Business etiquette*: Manners, listening, and business etiquette seem to have taken a backseat to profits, losses and restructuring these days, but in my experience, there is no substitute for these core disciplines when finding a sponsor. Sponsors put like with like; if they can't take you to a five-star restaurant, a ball game, a golf course, a Broadway play, or a sports bar, or introduce you to their family, how can they bring you into the sacred confines of the corporate boardroom—let alone set you up in the corner office next to theirs?

2. *Common sense*: There is no excuse for not using common sense, nor is there any substitute for it. It can't be taught at Harvard or Yale, no matter how many MBAs you earn. Common sense is the determining factor that takes someone who looks good on paper to the next level and makes them a good candidate for sponsorship.

3. *Style, substance, and sophistication*: The 3 Ss cannot be faked, copied, borrowed, or phoned in, as style, substance, and sophistication are the cornerstones of finding, securing, and fostering a successful sponsorship. The payoff for dressing and playing the part of a successful business executive is actually becoming a successful business executive!

4. *Extracurricular research*: Power brokers at the highest level of corporate success do not clock in at 9 a.m. and punch out at 5 p.m. Even if they are on-site a mere 40 hours per week, by no means does this mean that they only work 40 hours a week. Today deals are done everywhere: on golf courses, in airline VIP lounges, in press boxes, in the back booths of five-star restaurants, on plastic molded benches at fast-food restaurants, on-site, in the field, and everywhere in between. Knowing the business means knowing the players and what they like, dislike, and are absolutely passionate about. This is the subtle field known as "extracurricular research" and to secure the best possible sponsor, your extracurricular research should be second to none.

5. *What can you do for me?* Make it known that you are a team player, that you know playing the game at the top isn't easy, and that, most of all, you are eager and willing and will soon be able to give back to your sponsor. Have definitive plans for how to achieve that goal. Maybe you'll publish an article in the company newsletter naming your sponsor specifically, maybe you'll always remember to thank your sponsor as you move up; whatever it may be, you have to remember that your sponsor will want to look good through your job. Getting results is the best way to make your sponsor proud—not to mention make your sponsor look good!

Got a Sponsor—Now What?

So what happens once you find a sponsor? A sponsor will be there for the duration of your career, provided you do not lose focus on helping him or her win points at the all-important top of the game. Do not lose focus on the things that are helping that sponsor look good.

There are some sponsors who take it to the next level—friendship. I've been fortunate and blessed enough to have sponsors who have actually turned into friends.

The sponsorship relationship is a very intimate one. For better or worse, you are aligning yourself with someone who is likely to be very visible, influential, and known in the company. Having a sponsor without a network is like not having a sponsor at all; it's not just the sponsor you're courting, but everyone in the sponsor's network. No network, no connections—no payoff.

If you don't do your research, if you're not vigilant about who you're courting and what your sponsor's role is in the company itself, you could wind up aligning yourself with someone not very popular in the higher echelon or someone who might even be on the way out of employment with the company (and not by choice).

Such negative associations can do more harm than good.

I think it's important to note at this juncture in the book that not every manager, senior executive, or even CEO makes a good sponsor. The point is not to settle for the person with the highest rank or salary, but the person with the most integrity, connections, and influence in the company. The more you perform, the more you provide results, the more you make yourself open to opportunity, the more attractive you become to a potential sponsor. In many ways, it's like dating: we all want to make ourselves more attractive and, in return, find someone attractive.

In terms of voting power, finding the right sponsor is about courting the one with the most votes that count. In other words, you can have all the friends on the floor, head the Cheer Club, lead the league in strikeouts on your company softball team, and generally have the popular vote, but it's the electoral vote that really counts. In the most important election of your life, your sponsor is the decider.

Your sponsor is a game changer; if your sponsor says you are getting promoted, you get promoted. This is very much a capitalistic view of things. When you're in a corporation, it isn't a democracy about pleasing all your coworkers, managers, and subordinates—it is about having a relationship with the key decision maker, the one who has the most influence on your future in the company.

"Friend Request" Your Sponsor

Friendship combined with sponsorship is one of the most powerful combinations you could ever have in corporate America. That's a whole other level of success. That means the sponsor considers you as part of his or her family. And that means the sponsor is willing to do things for you and open up doors for you that you couldn't have imagined. So when you make a mistake—and you will make mistakes—you learn from that mistake, you move on, and you continue to help other people with what you've learned from your mistakesas well. That sponsor's going to be there to help you, coach you, and guide you through that mistake.

But some sponsors don't only want you because of what you can bring to them. There are some sponsors who are willing to take their investment in you beyond the workplace and invest in you personally, and develop a personal relationship. Those are the sponsorships that I have found have been the most beneficial to me.

Friendship with your sponsor is great, but don't leave this section thinking it's a must. Some sponsors are friends, some friends are sponsors—some friends aren't sponsors and some sponsors aren't friends. The corporate environment is one where you will enjoy many different relationships. However, they don't have to be the same in order to make it to the top.

If you haven't matured your sponsorship into a friendship, then, depending on the severity of the mistake, your sponsor may not choose to support you and may even cut you loose. In other words, your mistake can be fatal. That's the harsh reality of how you play the game at the top and how the game is played.

Sponsors Get as Good as They Give

Never forget that modern corporations are political places. Every effort is made to create a unified front that portrays power, privilege, and position. When you provide your sponsor with the opportunity to act progressively and openly foster inclusion, you help him or her as much as you help yourself.

When a sponsor takes you under his or her wing, that sponsor can shout it to the rooftops. That sponsor becomes invested in your success and his or her superiors, likewise, are eager to hear about "the new kid's" exploits and become equally invested in your success.

If you succeed, your sponsor looks good, even great. If you fail, the sponsor suffers guilt by association. Showing gratitude alone will not be enough to satisfy your sponsor. Since your success is intrinsically linked at this point, the more you succeed, the more your sponsor succeeds. And the more your sponsor succeeds, the more *you* succeed.

Managing Your Peers and Keeping Your "Enemies" Close

It's important to remember that sponsorship doesn't exist in a vacuum. No matter how big they might be, modern businesses are small communities where divisions, teams, and departments all work closely together. If you think you can hide a blossoming sponsorship, well, think again.

Your peers are an essential part of your success at any level, and when most of them are aware that you have a relationship with the boss that goes beyond your just reporting them to him or her, it sometimes creates friction and resistance in subtle ways that can affect getting your job done. Some of these peers even turn into enemies.

When peers are not getting along, most people with C-level executives as their sponsor usually have the tendency to let their ego get in the way. The executive being sponsored by the boss feels, "Why do I have to go out of my way in interacting with that other person?" Wrong!

In reality, this is when you should keep your enemies closer to you, not further away. You need to give the appearance that you are doing everything humanly possible to build a healthy relationship with the peers whom you are not in competition with and other members outside of the function or business you are associated with. You must stay close to those who might derail your sponsorship because, if you *don't* keep them close to you, you will not know what they are doing or thinking. In other words, you'll be working in the dark, and it's hard to react—or anticipate—when you're in the dark.

Also, you must not create issues for your boss (sponsor) because that puts him or her in the uncomfortable position of having to take time out to solve a dispute among direct reports. Some things you could do to manage your peers/enemies are to openly praise them or have them do a presentation to tell your staff what their teams are all about, what they are working on, and/or what they needs from you and your team to ensure they meet their strategic and financial objectives. Why not invite that person out to lunch? All of these moves put you in the power seat where you are managing your peers versus being on the defensive.

Those Who Keep Cool Rule

Do you remember when Tom Cruise jumped on Oprah's couch during an interview?

Of course you do; we all do. Such is the power of the emotional freak-out. And while most of us won't have the opportunity to do so on national television, keep in mind that companies are like mini

TV studios: what you do—and how you do it—are always being watched, analyzed, gossiped over, and mined for telltale signs about your ability to play at the top.

When you let your enemy see you sweat, or see you get emotional, it's a lose–lose proposition. Once enemies get an image in their mind of you in the midst of a freak-out, a bust out, a cut down, or a personal slip, it stays with them and tarnishes your image. It's sometimes hard to keep your cool, but they who keep cool rule.

In other words, never let yourself get so comfortable at work that you treat it like your living room, the gym, the movie theater, or even the front seat of your car. Those are emotional places, where you can laugh; cry; get irate, mad, or sad; or freak out. Work is not that place—at least, not if you want to play the game at the top.

Here are a few simple tips on keeping your cool in the workplace:

- *Keep it separate*: One of the biggest reasons many people get emotional at work is simply because they get so familiar there that they forget to keep their work lives and personal lives separate. This shouldn't dissuade you from loving your job, working overtime, or making your cubicle homey—just don't treat the workplace like your living room.

- *Your boss is not your mother (or father):* Debra Mandel, PhD, author of *Your Boss Is Not Your Mother*, explains how easy it is for us to put a personal face on our professional relationship. She explains, "We develop expectations of others that simply can't be met. We search for validation in all the wrong places, from all the wrong people. We want our boss or coworker to make up for the things that our mommy, daddy or sis never provided for us." When we treat our supervisors like parents, we can often react accordingly—that is, with too much emotion for the workplace.

- *Count to ten*: Counting to ten is an oldie but a goodie—or some of you may prefer the new terminology: Wusahhhh! When you feel pressure mounting; when you feel discouraged, disgraced, or disappointed; or when you feel the kettle steaming, back up and take a deep breath— at least emotionally—and count to ten in your head. This buys you time to think about the consequences of a tantrum, freak-out, or blowout.

Sponsorship Is a Two-way Street:
How to Ensure that You Don't Let Your Sponsor Down

The beauty of sponsorship is that it is a two-way street; this gives as much power to the person being sponsored as it does to the executive doing the sponsoring. Too often in business, we give away our power to those who would abuse it, ignore it, or even betray it. We align ourselves with bosses going nowhere or form alliances with partners who would take the credit for our hard work. This book equips readers with the skills they need to attract, secure, and enjoy a long-lasting, success-creating sponsorship with a worthy individual who can and will foster their success. There is true power in that knowledge.

By recognizing the qualities you bring to your half of the sponsorship equation, you can not only feel confident about your role in the benefactor affiliation but also add value to the sponsor–sponsored relationship yourself. You can also feel empowered to ensure that your sponsor lives up to his or her end of the bargain, a vital tool for fostering success in any two-sided relationship.

The greatest setback on your personal journey to success would be squandering an otherwise stellar sponsorship opportunity by letting your sponsor down before you ever get the chance to take full benefit of his or her assistance. How can this happen? It's possible in a variety of very realistic, very common ways.

For instance, you can let your guard down and treat the sponsorship as less than vital. You could slack off on your business etiquette and make your sponsor look bad. You could forget the "like with like" rule and become someone less attractive or desirable to your sponsors or, worse, to those to whom your sponsor would recommend you. You could say one thing and do another, get lazy in your position, and feel too entitled by the sudden perks of sponsorship to continue doing the great work that got you sponsored in the first place—any or all of these vital trespasses could forever damage the fragile and ongoing sponsorship.

How does one avoid these common sponsorship traps? The solution is simple: always be vigilant, always be attentive, and always, *always* be a person worthy of sponsorship. Meaning, you need to know what your worth and value are in any situation.

The Art of Giving Back:
When It's Time to Sponsor Someone Else

For the sponsorship model to work, it needs two things: people to sponsor and people to be sponsored. As one might imagine, the scale is bottom-heavy; there are many more people in entry- to mid-level positions who need to be sponsored than there are those available, let alone willing, to do the sponsoring at the executive levels. In that sense, everyone who has ever been sponsored, or even knows someone who was sponsored successfully, should step up and sponsor someone else, particularly in the minority community. We need to begin recruiting, training, and grooming people for those top spots, as they will inevitably become more open to all of us in coming years.

Action Plan for Finding a Sponsor

So, you need to find a sponsor, but don't know where to look? Rest easy. Here is a simple action plan you can follow to quickly and effectively identify the five candidates who are best suited to sponsor you at your workplace:

What if I told you that you didn't have to find a sponsor on your team, in your department, or even on your floor? What if you were free to look for a sponsor anywhere, at any time, in any department? The fact is, sponsorship comes in all shapes and sizes, and you really aren't restricted by rank or privilege when it comes to finding a sponsor.

Think about it: If you could pick five people in your entire company to sponsor you, to change your game, to help you to the top, who would they be? Don't worry about how high up they are, how intimidating this exercise may be, or with whom you have the most in common. Use the spaces below to list the top five candidates to be your sponsor at your company:

Candidate #1: _____

_____

Candidate #2: _____

_____

Candidate #3: _____

_____

_____

Candidate #4: _____

_____

Candidate #5: _____

_____

Now, armed with this list, what are you going to do about it? To make this action plan even more actionable, go down this list and find out everything you can about each person on it. Start a notebook on each person, or a spreadsheet, or a Word document—whatever it may be to keep track of your future sponsor's likes, dislikes, habits, traits, and so on.

But don't become a stalker! Just genuinely pursue an active interest in the people on your lists to determine if they're really the right sponsor for you. You may find, over time, that the names on this list change, or the order does, as you find out more and more about who might be just right to take you to the next level. For an electronic version of our sponsor scorecard or to receive assistance in identifying your sponsor, visit www.corporateclimb.net.

Rule #4

Dream Big—
They Can't Measure What's In Your Heart

O NCE UPON A TIME, PEOPLE TALKED ABOUT THEIR dreams. It was common fodder for inspirational wall posters, book titles, and audio CDs to talk about dreams, what they're made of, why they're important, and how big they should be. I don't see as many of those posters and book titles anymore.

Believe it or not, dreams are still a big part of playing the game at the top. We don't talk about them a lot anymore, because, for the most part, dreams are intangible (some in my business might call them a "soft skill"; I prefer to call them "essential skills"), but nearly every one of the top executives I've ever had the privilege of working with has been a big dreamer.

These are the cutting-edge people, the people who bring big ideas to the table—people like Steve Jobs, Bill Gates, Steve Harvey, Richard Branson, Magic Johnson, Michael Dell, and Jeff Bezos—the dreamers and doers who change the entire way we look at business today.

I think the reason we don't talk as much about dreaming anymore is because, for many people, it stops there—they have the dream but never do anything about it. All dreams are important, but the dreams that turn into success have one special ingredient that's missing in the dreams that stay dreams: action.

I'm sure many people look at Amazon.com today and think, "It's just a big website for selling stuff. I could have done that!" And maybe they could have done it; maybe they once had that dream. But what Amazon.com founder Jeff Bezos had was more than just a dream—he had a goal, an action plan, and a quantifiable, measurable means of turning that dream into action.

That's what all top performers do: They dream big and act to back it up.

Don't Deny Your Dreams, and Don't Squelch Your X-Factor

The next rule is to dream big. After all, no one can measure what's in your heart. This chapter is probably the one that will help you understand a little bit more about me, Fenorris, the person, and how dreaming played a role in the success that I have today and that I've had throughout my career.

So one of the things we'll talk about in this chapter are the intangibles, those things that corporate executives can't necessarily touch or even see. We'll talk about what they mean to you, your X-Factor.

The best setup for a realizable dream is for you to be a dreamer who is willing to act and who has the education to put that action into words. That's a formidable situation because while many people have one or the other, very few have both the dream itself and the willingness to act on that dream.

For instance, there might be a well-educated person who is incapable of making decisions simply because she waits for all the information to come in first. Or there may be a hothead who acts first and acts fast, but may not have the educational or intellectual background to inform his actions.

In referring to education, I am talking about a formal education or an education in life. A formal education is what you learn in school; a life education is what you learn on the streets, out in the real world, beyond the classroom. Preferably you have received both types of education.

Many people with life education can easily obtain a formal education just by sitting in a class, reading a book, and taking some tests. But it's often much harder for someone with a formal education to get a life education because it requires so much real living and so many practical life skills. In other words, you *can* get a formal education by reading a book, but life lessons are often only learned through years of trial and error.

When I say you need to put an education behind your dreams what I'm really saying is that formal training and a life education will help make your dreams a reality by putting those unique skills to good use.

So when you combine someone who has educational sophistication with the ability and willingness to act, you have found—or have become— someone truly worthy of playing the game at the top! To me, there is only one thing more important than an education—"The power and ability to DREAM BIG!"

Meeting the Influencers

From time to time, you meet influencers in your life. These influencers leave a lasting impression, for whatever reason, that stays with you from the start. Some of them you meet in childhood—a favorite teacher, aunt or uncle, neighbor, friend, foe, or even sibling or parent. Others you meet later in life, such as a romantic partner, mentor, professor, classmate, coworker, or boss.

Regardless of when you come across these influencers in your life, they tend to make a lasting impression because they come at just the right time for you to understand their message.

For instance, besides my mother and father, Gus Calbert was an educator who got me very focused on education from the third or fourth grade on throughout the rest of my life. He said, "You can be a great athlete, Fenorris, but if you don't get an education, you're going to be just a statistic." Those fateful words led me to excel in athletics but never forget about academics.

What he meant by my becoming a statistic, of course, was being just another athlete who focuses on sports to the exclusion of everything else. Oftentimes, those same athletes fail to realize the crushing odds against becoming successful in college, let alone professional, sports.

So what do they do after skipping class to shoot hoops, play football, or run track during their collegiate years? Where do they go when their athletic eligibility is over? Where do they go if they get hurt and haven't achieved a degree? The point is, without an education, Mr. Calbert was telling me, I could wind up just like so many before me from my neighborhood and beyond.

By far the biggest influence in my life, from a values, work ethic, compassion, and spirituality perspective, is my mom. I come from a family of ten, seven boys and three girls. My mom and dad both worked, but as you can probably imagine, to support seven boys and three girls, you need to make a lot of money in order to have a quality life. Unfortunately, my parents did not graduate from high school; they were Christian people who worked very hard to try to provide a quality life for the kids despite incredible odds and limited work expectations.

To put it bluntly, I grew up in the projects, which represent a very urban, underdeveloped, lowly, economic situation for the very poor and the very hopeless. I have to admit that, on some days, we were a little bit of both.

I would say that my parents probably made about $4,000 a year supporting ten kids—but this wasn't in the 1940s or 1950s, when that kind of money meant something; this was in the 1980s and 1990s, when $4,000 was $4,000. However, my mother was creative and a hard worker. She would get clothes from Goodwill or garage sales. The clothes that didn't fit, she would sell in her own yard sale and make money. But she ended up giving most of everything away to people who were—believe it or not—even poorer than we were. My mother had the biggest heart of anybody I've ever met in the world.

So you can imagine that, as a young kid, I spent a lot of time denying my reality and simply dreaming about what life could be like for me beyond the projects. My mom made me feel special and taught all her kids that they could do whatever they wanted to through hard work, authenticity, honesty, and sincere effort. I was fortunate to have her and many other influencers in my life.

One of my favorite groups of influencers was the Olsson family from Grand Rapids, Michigan. This was a very affluent family, one who didn't come from the projects and who certainly made more than $4,000 a year. They helped me dream big.

The Olssons taught me that anything is possible, and they taught me about the X-Factor. They taught me how to invest and save money. They gave me another view of the world and what could be. Mr. Olsson treated my just like his son Jeff. Jeff and I were best buddies, and we played AAU basketball from the time we were in the ninth grade until we both went off to college. The Olssons helped me understand various aspects of dreaming by the life they lived not just by the things they owned. It wasn't just about dreaming for money, they explained. It was about dreaming about the type of life that I wanted as it relates to how I treated my wife and my kids, what type of things I wanted to expose my kids to, what charities I wanted to donate to, and who I wanted to help along the way.

Who Are Your Influencers?

It's important to have influencers in your life. I had people like Mr. Calbert, who helped me value education; my mother, who helped me value my spirituality, giving back, and a work ethic; and the Olssons, who helped me value my dreams. (There have been many more influencers since then as well.) But who are your influencers? Chances are, the names of one or two people who inspired you came to mind quickly—a former or current teacher, coach, spouse, friend, neighbor, or hero.

I encourage you to identify your influencers because they are valuable to your success, not just in business but also as a human being. In fact, that's the beauty of influencers—they don't have to fall into any particular category.

You may not consider a teacher on the same level as a businessperson-type mentor but, in fact, teachers are often our first influencers because they are the first people we spend lots of time with outside of our own home (and especially in childhood, when so many of us are influenced by teachers). What's more, teachers do more than just teach—they lead by example.

So many of the best influencers do. Consider my mom, for example—she was quick with a piece of advice, a piece of scripture, or a piece of life wisdom, but more than anything, we learned by the example she led in day-to-day life. Just her bearing, her indomitable will, and her refusal to buckle, even during what seemed like insurmountable odds, helped me overcome professional and personal obstacles in my own life as well.

Many of us are unintentional know-it-alls, and I don't mean that in a bad way. It's easy to get into that role of seeing is believing, of thinking that your way is the right way simply because it's the only way you know. The best influencers show you that there is another way, that change can be for the good, and that maybe you don't know it all.

For instance, back when Mr. Calbert warned me about becoming another statistic back in elementary school, I could have been knocked over with a feather. I was absolutely convinced that sports was my future, no ifs, ands, or buts. I just *knew* I would play pro ball and come back to town a millionaire someday. Well, I didn't play pro ball, but though not in the way I expected, I did come back a millionaire—and all because Mr. Calbert reminded me to keep an eye on my grades as well as the basket.

What's more, Mr. Calbert never said, "Fenorris, quit sports, do not play sports, stop playing sports." He knew better; he knew that for a kid in the projects with the right attitude, sports could be a way out of poverty and hopelessness.

He just wanted to give me the right attitude, put me in the right mindset. He did, and look what sports did for me. All those leadership, management, and organizational skills that helped me early on in my career were a direct result of sports. They were also a direct reflection of my commitment to educational excellence, thanks to one of my biggest life influencers.

So before you continue, take the time to list your top five influencers. Next to each influencer, write a brief explanation of why you're including that person on this list:

Influencer #1 _____

_____

Influencer #2 _____

_____

Influencer #3 _____

_____

Influencer #4 _____

_____

Influencer #5 _____

_____

The Power of Dreams

- What is your will?
- What are your circumstances?
- What are some of the things that are motivating you and driving you to have the type of success that you want, whatever it may be (as long as it's legal, of course)?

These were the questions I learned to ask myself at various junctures along my path to success. Thanks to positive influences I had in my youth, I learned to examine daily where I was in life and determine whether I was living my current dream. And so, dreaming big for me, as a child, was very, very important—it still is. In fact, dreaming has played a huge role in my success ever since childhood.

I know that if it weren't for dreaming I would not be where I am today. And I personally believe there's only one thing that's more important than an education, and that's the power and freedom of dreaming. If you're allowed to dream, you act upon your dream, and you put together a plan to build on that dream, you can achieve any goal you set out for yourself.

And I believed in that. I had a plan—a short-term dream, a mid-term focus, and a long-term focus. And when you actually take the time to write your dreams down, there's a better chance of achieving your dreams as opposed to just dreaming and not putting any plan together to accomplish your dream.

Remember, that's where action comes in. A dream without action is just a daydream; a dream *with* action is a dream that springs to life and affects all your days forevermore.

My Big Dream: From Daydreamer to Do-Dreamer

Growing up in poverty wasn't easy. Seven brothers and three sisters—that's a lot of mouths to feed if you're making $40,000 a year, let alone a tenth as much! I loved my family; I still do, and always will.

But there was another family that helped shape my future, and to them I also owe a debt. The Olsson family helped shape my dream and helped make me want to bring my dream to reality in a way that was practical, doable, measurable, and all-too-achievable. The Olssons were not daydreamers; they were do-dreamers.

What do I mean by do-dreaming? You have dreamers; people who dream but don't do. Then you have doers; people who do but don't dream. I learned the art of do-dreaming, which is adding action to your dreams to make them become a reality.

The Three Vital Habits of Do-Dreamers

Are you a daydreamer or a do-dreamer? To help you figure it out, following are the three vital habits of do-dreamers:

1. *They dream the right dreams:* What do I mean by dreaming the right dream? Listen, we all have daydreams. We want to be sports stars, rock stars, movie stars, supermodels, and millionaires. And I'm not saying those dreams aren't the right dreams for somebody, but are they the right dream for you? Making a dream come true isn't all about the payoff—a lot of it has to do with the plan. So right away, you need to determine which dream is right for you, because if you spend hours, days, weeks, months, and even years planning for the wrong dream for you, you're going to be wasting your time. So be realistic. Maybe you're not a movie star, but you're a character actor; maybe you're not a quarterback, but you're a defensive lineman; and maybe you're a fashion designer, but not a supermodel. All dreams are the right dreams if they're the right dreams for *you*.

2. *They dream and do equally:* Do-dreamers don't do too much and dream too little, or dream too much and do too little. Instead, they do equal parts of both—and that makes all the difference. We all know people who dream too much—they

dream so much, so often, that they can barely get out of bed let alone achieve their dreams. Yet those who do, and only do, are just as bad. They perform a variety of tasks with no apparent goal in mind other than completing that goal and then moving on to the next. Do-dreamers assign status to their goals, prioritize them, and do them in order to achieve their goal. If their dream is to act, they make every goal geared toward acting; they read screenplays or books on acting, watch movies with a critical eye, and rehearse, rehearse, rehearse. Athletes who are do-dreamers do everything in sight of their dream; they work out regularly, devour coaching manuals, memorize playbooks, hang out with other athletes, watch sports, eat right, and so on. This reflects the "like with like" idea: Do-dreamers do and dream in equal parts so that every aspect of their life is built around either doing or dreaming, not one or the other.

3. *They never, ever give up:* Do-dreamers have already made their dream a part of their reality. They may not have become an actor, played pro sports, or gotten the corner office, but they have been dreaming and doing so long that they might as well have. So those dreams, those actions on behalf of their dreams, are enough to keep them going even when times are tough. And, fortunately, those day-to-day efforts on behalf of their dreams are what keep do-dreamers going, even when times are tough and when their dreams seem so very, very out of reach. As a result of always doing, of always dreaming, do-dreamers never, ever, *ever* give up!

By teaching me the art of do-dreaming, the Olssons helped me understand that this dream that I have could actually, with hard work, become a reality. By doing and dreaming, I could have both the dream and the means to achieve it. And keep in mind, thanks to the Olssons and all my other influencers, it was more than just a dream about making money.

These people taught me that who you are is what you do, and that no amount of money can make you something better than you already are. Learning that valuable life lesson early helped me focus my priorities not just on making money but also on making a success of myself.

Dreaming for me was key. Out of all the things that have motivated me to achieve the level of success that I have, dreaming big and doing just as big was probably, in fact, the most important criterion to achieving the success that I've had in my career.

Dreams were big but, for the Olssons, and later for me, goals (that is, the "doing" part of being a do-dreamer) became even bigger. If dreams are the seeds we plant hoping they become a beautiful, radiant flower, then goals are the water we use to grow them to maturity, and the way we care for them and feed them until they mature and become, for us, a living, breathing reality.

The greatest success one can ever imagine, beyond money, beyond fame, beyond big houses and fancy cars, is to see one's dream become a reality. Fortunately, becoming a do-dreamer gives you the tools it takes to make your dreams come true.

See It to Achieve It

Many people feel their dreams but never see them. That is, they have this dream that's been there for as long as they can remember, and it may drive them forward and propel them into a certain career or track in school, but if they never actually visualize themselves living the dream, if they never quite see it come true, well, then that dream will always stay just a dream.

If you expect to achieve something, but you can't see it, then it's probably going to be very difficult, if not impossible, for you to achieve that goal. Visualization is key to achieving your dreams—not just in a new age, self-help way but in a very real, very doable, and very achievable way.

You simply *have* to see it before you can achieve it. That's a model that I've always used throughout my career. When I interviewed first for Motorola and then Dell, I had pictured the interview in my head so often, for so long, that it was like it had already happened, like it was déjà vu when I sat down to conduct the interview.

Visualizing is not just staring off into space and watching yourself drive off into the sunset in a Rolls-Royce. It's about what you see before any of that ever happens. Visualization is far from glamorous; when I visualize it's like seeing a conference call in 3-D. I'm picturing the setting a meeting will be in, or what a new product might look like, or how many pages of blueprints there might be, or even how many clients might be in on an acquisitions and merger meeting.

Yet, as mundane as they seem, these pictures in my head are actually helping me achieve my overall dream of playing at the top. Knowing these details, playing out the scenarios, and trouble-shooting this or that potential crisis allows me to dream bigger and do more because even though I'm often surprised, I'm never quite so surprised that I can't respond quickly. Why? Because I've already visualized myself succeeding during this very type of crisis, and so I am doubly prepared to address it when it finally happens.

Seeing something, even though it's not there, and being able to visualize it, is only half the battle. Even when the mental picture you visualize is so beautiful it can leave you breathless (or bring you to tears), you have to be willing to put in the work and the time to achieve it.

Now, you and I both know that there are some people out there who are not willing to put in the time. There are some people who want to cut corners and achieve things quickly. But no long-term success can be achieved by cutting corners.

Steve Harvey: The Ultimate Do-Dreamer

I've been fortunate enough to know people who've had dreams and who, through hard work and do-dreaming, have achieved those dreams. One such gentleman is my friend Steve Harvey.

Steve Harvey is one of the leading radio personalities in the United States today. In fact, he has about 8 million listeners, and Steve talks about his dream quite openly. One of the things that Steve dreamed about early on was achieving a level of success from being a comedian and, more than that, being the best person that he could be.

Steve talks a lot about how people tried to deny him his dream by telling him that he wasn't smart enough. And it was the people he loved who told him that. People he respected told him he didn't have what it takes to be a successful comedian, and they never, ever dreamed that he would have one of the most popular radio shows in the United States.

Steve's dream started in Cleveland, Ohio. He grew up very poor. Steve spent many nights in the family car, trying to figure out when he was going to get someplace warm to sleep or have a hot shower or how he was going to get clothes when it got cold. Steve later worked at a GM car factory, making cars and providing parts. But he had this dream. And he didn't let it stop him. The success that Steve has now required a dream, and not just seeing it, but believing in himself and doing what it took to make his dream a reality.

Steve was obviously a do-dreamer, but he also had the X-Factor— that intangible quality that made him persevere, keep dreaming, keep doing, and achieve his goal, his dream, even when the people he loved the most told him he wasn't good enough, wasn't smart enough, to see his dreams come true.

The X-Factor is not just your dream but your willingness to believe in your dream—in yourself—even when nobody else does, even when all the signs are pointing against your success, and even when absolutely nobody is holding out a hand to help.

Do you see how being a do-dreamer or having that X-Factor is an intangible quality that people can't really see on paper? Yet, they can see it if they look closely enough; I try to look closely enough. And if you have any kind of success in this world, it's often because enough people along the way looked closely enough to see that X-Factor in you.

Someone had to give you a chance along the way. For me, it was my influencers and, later, my sponsor. For Steve Harvey it was everyone who ever booked him in a comedy club or chose to be his manager or play his radio show. Who will it be for you? Who will notice your X-Factor and, more importantly, how will you get them to notice it?

The X-Factor Starts with Me, Myself, and I

Not surprisingly, it all starts with you. Whether you're in corporate America or you're an entrepreneur, whether you're an actor or an athlete, it's really hard to expect anyone else to believe in what you're selling if *you* don't believe in yourself first. Most people who are dreaming are selling something about themselves.

You're the commodity, and like any good salesperson, you have to first believe in yourself to sell that commodity to anyone else. (Heck, they sure aren't going to give it to you!) If you don't believe in yourself, no one else will. So, it's more than just having a dream—it's about believing in that dream even when nobody else on the planet will believe in it with you.

There are times along your path to the top where you will feel very, very alone. In corporate America, self-preservation is key, and so it doesn't behoove others to cheer you on or form your unofficial pep squad.

In fact, quite the opposite is true. In corporate America, you will find an entire subculture of doom-and-gloomers who will shoot down every idea you ever have, who will make you prove everything to them time and time again, and who will openly wish for you to fail at every single opportunity there is to do so. You will read more about these corporate enemies later in this book, but for now, just know that they exist and that they are very, very discouraging.

But this happens only if you let them discourage you. The power of self-belief is that it is kryptonite to the doom-and-gloomers, who hate people who believe in themselves because so few of them are capable of it.

Unfortunately, the more others doubt you, the easier it is to believe them. You must stay strong and ignore them. Believe in yourself long enough, strong enough, and often enough, and others will eventually believe in you as well.

You have to be able to visualize it, and then you have to be willing to put in the work to achieve it. This formula will make believers of the doubters, even if one of them is *you*. That means going over, and sometimes around, obstacles, because you will have obstacles.

As Steve Harvey and I found out the hard way, and as you one day surely will, not everyone is necessarily cheering for your success. Not everyone necessarily believes in your dream.

The only thing that matters in the end is that you believe in your dream. And if you believe in your dream and you're willing to work to become a do-dreamer instead of a daydreamer, then you're going to have a better chance of achieving your dream.

My X-Factor

So you may ask, "How do I discover my X-Factor? And what is my X-Factor?" My simple answer is that life is too short to do things that don't help you become a better person. And in order to become better yourself, it is vital to surround yourself with people who will help you become a better person.

As you think about your own X-Factor—or if you're discovering your X-Factor for perhaps the very first time (although likely you will have been dreaming about it for years)—consider this perspective: if money were no object, what kind of work would you do even knowing that you wouldn't get paid for it? In other words, what would you do for free?

That's how I discovered my X-Factor, which is working with people and building teams: being able to take teams that were mediocre—whether it was in sports or in the high-level departments in *Fortune* 50 companies—and turn them around so that they could meet the expectations of those who depended on them, be it coaches, the fan in the stands, direct supervisors, the CEO, or even customers.

Team building, team leading, team formatting, team selection, team streamlining—show me a team, and I can craft it to become something better than the sum of its parts.

That's my passion, my X-Factor. I would do that even if I weren't getting paid, because I simply love doing it. There's something about watching something develop in accordance with what I have designated for it that makes my life worthwhile.

Teams aren't easy to control, and anyone who has ever led a team knows that. But that is the personal challenge to me: taking a team and integrating all of the players so that rather than working against each other, they end up working like a well-oiled machine. That is my personal challenge and my professional challenge, and as I've said, I'd do it at night, on the weekends, in my spare time—and for free—if I had to.

My X-Factor was, at the time, pleasing my superiors, helping them to understand that when they gave me an assignment, they didn't have to think about whether or not it was going to get done. They knew it was going to get done, plain and simple. And that knowledge allowed them to think about other aspects of their business and not have to constantly worry and micromanage me or my team.

Some might see leading a team as a thankless job, but in fact, it's quite rewarding because the more people can rely on you, the more jobs you can get done with the least amount of supervision possible, and the more you directly affect a supervisor's life because he or she doesn't have to worry about you!

So if I can take a challenging team and turn it around, if I can take that pressure away from my boss, if I can turn a rowdy team quiet or an unproductive team productive, I have given my boss two gifts. First, the boss doesn't have to worry about that team anymore; it's another headache. Second, the work gets done and productivity instantly turns around. What was once a weakness is now a strength, and who do they thank for those gifts? Me, that's who.

That's the beauty of the X-Factor. When you really love to do something—and would even do it for free—that enthusiasm is blatantly apparent to anyone. People can see enthusiasm—it's obvious to those who hire you, employ you, supervise you, and pay you. And when that enthusiasm produces results, your X-Factor makes you a specialist.

Now, I realize not everybody gets crazy-excited about organizational development, but that's even better! When your X-Factor is in a field that allows you to specialize, that makes you a big fish in a small pond and an even bigger target when your superiors are looking for relief.

Something else that put my superiors at ease was that they knew that the way I carried myself, from a presentation standpoint, from reporting to higher-ups, and from dealing with C-level executives, I would represent them well. And remember, superiors love it when you make them look good.

So not only was I getting results, taking pressure off them, and turning challenges into rewards, but I could also stand up for them in a team meeting or departmental focus group and represent them well. My X-Factor was worth something to them.

The X-Factor is important because it signifies excellence. When you engage in your X-Factor, when you are lucky enough to do it for a living, you are going to be so happy to be doing it, so grateful to be allowed to do it, and so jazzed about simply doing it that the end result will now and forever be excellence.

And excellence appeals to you, to your superiors, to your executives, to your team members, and especially to your sponsors. My supervisors knew that if something had to do with team building, productivity, and efficiency, they could give it to me, and because it was my X-Factor, it would be done with excellence. That attracted sponsors and helped my dreams come true beyond my wildest imagination.

In short, when you determine your X-Factor and are finally allowed to apply it to what you do, you become the ultimate problem solver. If your X-Factor is technology, you can be the person who fixes those technical glitches that nobody else seems to know what to do about. When your X-Factor is marketing and promotions, you become the go-to person for bright, new, unique, yet practical ideas that boost sales by significant percentages. When R & D is your X-Factor, you become the person to whom the whole company looks for game-changing strategies to take the organization into the future.

In other words, everybody loves an expert. And knowing, living, and learning your X-Factor makes you an expert—in yourself.

Why Does the X Factor Matter?

You may also be wondering why someone should care about an X-Factor. I mean, isn't just working hard, showing up, and sometimes staying late enough? In some companies, sure; in others, that's not even enough to keep your job, let alone get to the top. The X-Factor is that difference between a job and a career, between mediocrity and superiority, and between showing up and going the extra mile. Think about the hundreds of thousands of people who have MBAs or who are going to school for MBAs, and consider today's economy and that people are losing their jobs. That means less opportunity for people who have MBAs or are close to earning their MBAs. So the X-Factor is even more critical in this competitive, struggling economy.

In other words, those with an X-Factor shine, and executives want to hire people who shine, regardless of what other skills they may possess. Maybe you are a diehard techie who doesn't have his MBA, who dresses a little odd and who isn't that adept at social situations— *but* you love what you do so much that you practically wear your X-Factor like a superhero costume.

Don't you think the person who leaps off the page with enthusiasm and expertise is going to appeal to an HR representative more than someone who dresses the part but can't be bothered to get excited about his or her potential job? Shine, and the world takes notice; and the X-Factor helps you shine. Supervisors want to promote people who shine, who are excellent, who deliver, who get results, and who do all that with enthusiasm.

People who are able to articulate the X-Factor beyond their résumé are people who are probably going to have a leading edge over people who just went to school and all they have to talk about is an MBA.

Never underestimate the power of good, old-fashioned enthusiasm; although it isn't enough in itself to get you the job, enthusiasm—almost more than anything else—helps you jump off the page and turn an impersonal interview personal. And personal is what personnel is all about!

Think about enthusiasm from the interviewer's standpoint. If you're doing interviews all day long, all week long, all month long, and the same kinds of people with the same pedigrees from the same Ivy League colleges come in and all they can talk about are their GPAs and their MBAs and their valedictorian speeches. And then another person comes in, a passionate person who can talk about teamwork, real-life experience, and getting results because of his or her X-Factor. Well, who would *you* hire?

A lot of things discussed in this chapter will help you position yourself at getting a job offer from an X-Factor perspective. Understanding the value of having an X-Factor can help show you what your X-Factor is, and this will help better position yourself to get the job over someone who doesn't have an X-Factor.

Becoming a VP

Becoming a VP is not easy. I don't want anyone to misconstrue that what I'm talking about in these chapters is going to automatically get you right up to the level of VP in any of the biggest companies in the world.

There were quite a few X-Factors in play for me when I became a VP. I want to be as transparent as I can here: it was a favor. Favor is a spiritual term from the Bible. I firmly believe that God has bestowed favor on my life. I am truly blessed.

Someone saw something in me. Someone saw in me, without my necessarily talking about it, the environment I came from. This person knew that the odds were stacked against me and that I had earned a master's degree and played sports. This person was willing to take a chance and bet on me.

Basically, that's what sponsorship is all about. Someone who is willing to make a bet that you're going to come through and help him or her win, and just as important, you're going to help yourself win. Winning is being able to put yourself in the position where you can achieve financial success that can change your life and, I think just as important, change other people's lives.

Remember: like with like. Most people at the top know their X-Factor and live it every day. Work is long and stressful and occasionally boring, unless you have an X-Factor. So those at the top (who already have an X-Factor) want to work with others who have X-Factors and are actively on the lookout for those enthusiastic people with a mission beyond just showing up to work and retiring early.

And since so few people know their X-Factor, let alone convey it to others, when potential sponsors, VPs, CEOs, or other C-level executives spot someone with an X-Factor who can make their professional lives easier and make their work lives more interesting, they are going to campaign actively on behalf of that person's success, if not sponsor that person outright.

Conveying Your X-Factor

Timing is critical in being able to read the unspoken X-Factor. If you spend a lot of time with MBA students or people who have master's degrees, you might want to talk about how you have your MBA or master's degree because you are excited about it, and you should be. However, I strongly encourage that whenever possible—and it's *always* possible— you do more listening than talking.

As I just mentioned, it's all about timing. There will be a time when you have sought out someone who you think could either be your mentor or sponsor, someone who can do something big for your game, change it in a way that alters your destiny forever, where you'll have an opportunity to talk about yourself.

And you'll get the opportunity to talk about yourself in a way where it doesn't seem like you're bragging or self-promoting—in a situation when that potential mentor or sponsor will just want to know about you. I've had those situations happen to me, where I've waited for the right time. The timing is something that you have to be able to establish.

You have to allow that person to understand you—the real you. You want him or her to walk away really understanding what makes you tick beyond your grades, beyond what you've accomplished at school. What is your X-Factor? And why should he or she care? Ask yourself: Does your MBA make you, or does your life experience make you? My master's degree didn't make me. It was my life experiences that connected with the sponsor. That is something that will help give you the X-Factor when you connect beyond the MBA because, as I've said, a lot of people have MBAs. The X-Factor is what connects you to that person on a level beyond the fact that you're some smart brainiac kid who has all the answers to the corporation's problems.

A sponsor knows you don't have the answers to the company's problems—at least, not yet. That takes time. Instead, you need to connect on a personal level. And there will be a time where you are going to get that opportunity, and the question for you is: "Will you be ready to connect with that sponsor and demonstrate your X-Factor?"

And before you answer that question, you have to answer this: what *is* your X-Factor?

Let Your X-Factor Take the Driver's Seat

When you think about your X-Factor, the question should be, "How will my X-Factor drive me?"

Success for me was not about making all the money I could. Making money is important, sure, if you have a dream. It takes money to succeed in this world, if only because money allows you the time, motivation, and opportunity to succeed. But what my X-Factor *really* gave me was the ability to be able to put myself in a position where I could go from success to significance.

A Lasting Legacy Starts with You

More than anything, I wanted to be in a position where I could take my success, the success of being a vice president in two of the biggest companies in the world—*Fortune* 50 companies—before I was 40, and leverage that success to help others, because that's the legacy that I wanted to leave.

I believe that there is no finish line to success—success is ever-evolving, ever-changing, and in the best of scenarios, everlasting. Success is also not an individual endeavor but a collective enterprise;

you are not alone in success. You weren't alone in succeeding in the first place, and you shouldn't be alone in spending your riches.

Yes, we all want to think we got to the top by ourselves, but I don't know anyone who is actually at the top who believes that. Everyone had a sponsor somewhere along the way. Even if you started your own company as the founder and CEO, who gave you your first chance? Who was your first customer? Who loaned you the first dollar?

Was it your dad, who let you use the garage to build your first computer? Was it your mom, who invested her retirement account in your crazy idea? Was it a favorite uncle, who cosigned your first loan? Maybe it was a neighbor who had an empty warehouse and let you rent it for a song to afford you the opportunity to meet that first order and start your career.

Even if we have to travel far downstream to locate the origins of our success, I believe we all got some help when we needed it the most. It could have been a scholarship to the best business school in the country, an introduction to the most important person in the company you want to work for, a chance encounter with your favorite business author, or a referral to an angel fund investor. Whatever the case may be, whenever it happened or whoever it was, without sponsors of some sort, none of us would be here, and indeed, few of us would ever succeed.

I believe that because someone sponsored me and gave me an advantage, I should turn around and do the same thing for someone else. None of us lives on an island; we are all in this together. To truly succeed, you must help others when and where you can. That, to me, is the true definition of success.

I don't want my kids and people who know me to remember me simply as, "Fenorris, who was the VP at Motorola and Dell," or "Fenorris, who started his own company," or even, "Fenorris, who wrote a book." Quite frankly, that would be very boring. I want my success and my legacy to be about the significance of my life.

Remember how earlier I said that success doesn't have a finish line? That the finish line keeps moving with every subsequent success? That the minute we think we're done, we really are?

Well, no matter how successful you are, to me, if you're not sharing that success, if you're not extending a hand to someone on the way up, you may have all the success and riches and cars and homes and titles and accomplishments and sycophants and accolades in the world but, ultimately, that success is a hollow thing, indeed.

Answering the Big Questions

I wrote earlier that your X-Factor is that thing you are so jazzed about that you would do it even if nobody paid you for the privilege. But those of us who are fortunate to have, identify, and live our X-Factor also owe the world a payback for the privilege of being able to live our dreams.

So when you stop to think about your X-Factor, don't ignore the big questions—questions like:

- Did I make a difference in other people's lives?
- What difference did I make for someone who may have grown up without many advantages?
- What difference did I make to aspiring people who have just finished an MBAs or a master's degree in trying to achieve a certain level of success that they've dreamed about?
- What difference will I make in my life?
- How will I be remembered?
- Did my success make a difference in the lives of others?
- Will someone else succeed because of me?
- Will I be able to play an active, or even silent, role in that success?
- How much can I afford to help?
- How many people can I help—and how often?

Remember, none of us is in this alone, and if you're the kind of person who does have an X-Factor, who gets excited about work for work's sake, you will also likely be the kind of person who can't wait to give back to others once you finally achieve a modicum of success for yourself. Much like your X-Factor, helping others succeed is equally addictive.

What will your X-Factor help you create? The next Action Plan should help.

X-Factor Action Plan:
Committing to Your X-Factor

I had an X-Factor that I was going to make teams productive; that was my dream. Steve Harvey had an X-Factor that he was going to be the best comedian he could be. That was his dream.

Now it's time to come to terms with your dream, with your X-Factor. What I can say to you about that very important subject is this: only *you* can achieve your dreams. A mentor can help, a sponsor can pave the way, and a promotion can get you up that next rung, but it's you who has to cross the finish line.

Many people read books like this and say, "Hmm, that was interesting. I think I'll do that." But I don't want you to just think about this book, these ideas, or my experiences and then never do anything with what you've learned. Instead, I want you to succeed. I want you to play the game at the top, but the only way to do that is to take your career by the reins and really hold on tight the whole way there.

So many people lose sight of their dreams. I admit, I was tempted many times to do the same. It is hard out here, and the higher you get up the ladder, the harder and harder it gets. But if that is what you want in life, you have to be prepared for it, and that is what I am trying to do by spending so much time getting you to think about the X-Factor.

Now I'm going to give you an opportunity to share a secret that you've never shared with anybody before: What is your X-Factor? You know what it is.

To be the CEO of Microsoft, to work in Silicon Valley, to own your own company, to invent the next big running shoe, to write a best-selling book, to consult to *Fortune* 50 companies—whatever that dream is, you know it. I know you do. So now is your chance to own it; to admit it, once and for all, outside of your private thoughts; and to commit to it, no ifs, ands, or buts, until you achieve it.

On the lines provided below, I want you to write your X-Factor. Dare to dream.

_____

_____

_____

_____

_____

_____

Now, I want you to commit to that dream. You don't have to do so out loud, though it helps. You don't even have to tell anyone else about this little exercise, though it helps. As long as you know your X-Factor, as long as you commit to your dream, no one can take that away from you.

No one, that is, except you. You know what it will take to reach your goals. I've shared those requirements with you already: see your dream, find your vision, make your plan, and stick with it. It's what I did, it's what Steve Harvey did, and it's what tens of thousands of dream-makers have done.

Now it's your turn...

Rule #5

Forging Alliances—Popular Vote vs. Electoral Vote

BACK IN 2000, VICE PRESIDENT AL GORE TOOK ON Texas governor George W. Bush in a heated battle to become our next president of the United States. And as we all know by now, the final results were that Al Gore finished with the most popular votes. In other words, more citizens voted for Al Gore to become our next president than for George Bush.

Cause for celebration? Well, not so fast. That's because George Bush won the *actual* presidency of the United States. Huh? What? How? Simple: He won the most electoral votes. More of the people whose votes actually counted threw their votes behind Bush.

In politics as in life, we all want to be popular, and we all want to be liked. But for many of us in the workplace, it goes beyond being well-liked to being well-compensated. We equate being the most popular with being the most valuable, but more than just in terms of quantity, we have to think of the quality of our popularity.

Just whom, in other words, are we popular with? You may be the junior executive who can claim the best working relationships with the sanitation department, the secretarial pool, or even HR, but ask yourself: "How is this going to help get me to the *top*?"

I'm not saying that every relationship you have *has* to be mercenary, but it *is* important when spending time with coworkers that you spend the right time with the right people.

It all comes back to this overarching theme of putting like with like. If you're going to the top, shouldn't you associate with other people on the way up? Everyone should be friendly, courteous, and professional at work, but not every relationship is going to be a stepping-stone to the top.

In corporate America, most people get caught up with trying to have the most votes from a popularity perspective as opposed to a quality perspective. They naively assume that the most popular wins when such is not often the case. In fact, it is rarely the case. In corporate America, there are only one or two votes that really matter.

These are the alliances you should be concerned with the most.

You Can Lose Even if You've Got the Popular Vote

One of your first instincts as a new or entry-level employee, or even when you're gunning for that new promotion or a kick-start to your current employment status, is to go out of your way to make everybody happy. It's human nature to want to be liked, to want to make people happy, to want to please others, and to actively covet their affection.

I've seen too many people focus on trying to be Mr. or Ms. Popularity and, in the process, lose focus on what really matters. And what really matters is helping the company win market share and getting results that turn into profits.

How does your popularity benefit the company? How does it increase production? How does it supercharge your productivity?

The short answer is that it doesn't. Your supervisor doesn't need you to be the most popular person in the plant, in the office, or in your cubicle cluster. Your supervisor and your supervisor's supervisor and on up the line need you to be the most consistently productive and performing person in the plant, the office, or your cubicle cluster. That is what gets results and helps your company win; that is what earns you the most "electorate" votes, that is, the one or two or possibly three votes that really count.

This is not to say you should shut out your friends in other departments, or spend time exclusively with your own team, even if those people are the biggest bores on the planet!

This *is* to say that you need to at least prioritize your time so that you can spend just enough time with those workplace relationships that don't really move you forward and even more time with the people whose relationships can change your game and your life.

Winning: A Definition You Can Get Behind

Before you can start to win, you need to define your terms for winning. If getting to the top means being the most liked, then work really *will* become a popularity contest. But that's not why you're reading this book and that's definitely not how you'll make it to the top. You're reading this book to get to the top, and the alliances you'll need to make it to the top are not necessarily those that are the most popular.

In other words, focus on the electoral vote, not the popular vote. You really need to identify the few people are who matter most to your ability to help your career progress and focus on creating relationships, in the form of alliances, with them.

This doesn't have to happen to the exclusion of the popular vote; some people just light up an office and, if that's you, more power to you. By all means, be popular, as long as it doesn't affect the time you spend with those in the company whose votes really matter. But don't settle for mere popularity—make the electorate vote your priority.

Management Versus Growth: The Two Phases of Your Career

Most of us see our careers as one long arc, with a beginning, a middle, and an end. But when it comes to getting to the top of any company or organization, there are really two distinct phases of your career: managing your career and growing your career.

1. *Managing your career:* In the career management phase, you are primarily concerned with getting your bearings (in a new job or position), keeping up with supply and demand, mastering your job skills, making sure your supervisors are happy, and getting along with your team. You're not quite ready to grow your career yet because you're still getting a handle on it and haven't yet cemented your expertise or X-Factor.

2. *Growing your career:* In the career growth phase, however, you have essentially mastered your goal, made your superiors happy, are fluent in team dynamics, and have gotten to a place where you have more time and energy to devote to your future. This is when you can start to take a step back from your day-to-day duties and analyze where you want to go next, how you can get there, and what being there actually means.

Which of these two phases is more important? Well, that's like asking which came first, the chicken or the egg? Frankly, just like the chicken or the egg, you can't have one without the other.

For you to manage your career, you have to have the kind of devotion and motivation it takes to grow your career. And for you to get to the point where career growth becomes a concern, you have to have your basic career management skills down. In other words, you have to walk before you can run!

Compare this idea to exercising. If you've never gone to a gym, your first few weeks there can be exhausting, blinding, sweaty, and not very fulfilling. You feel like you'll never get the hang of this machine or that, and it doesn't feel like you're getting any stronger, lighter, bigger, or whatever you joined the gym for in the first place. You come close to giving up, but you stick with it.

Fast forward to the third or fourth week of your gym membership, and finally, you're getting the hang of things. You know the best time to go so it's not too crowded, you know the machines that fit your personality and strengths, you're finally starting to see some muscle tone, you've got good breath control, and you're not so sweaty. Finally, you're actually starting to think, you could probably ride this stationary cycle for ten more minutes tonight or maybe you should add some barbells to the weight bench, because your routine is getting a little too easy." In short, you've gone from *managing* your health to *growing* it; now you can focus on things like building more muscle, strengthening for tone, and so on.

Work is a lot like that. A brand new job, promotion, title, or opportunity can feel hectic, frantic, and sometimes even out of control—but once you get the hang of things, once you've managed those first few weeks or months, the pace slows down, you're able to do more with less, and your mind starts to think about what comes next.

And what comes next, of course, is growth.

What Comes Next: Get the Right Electoral Votes

When it comes to getting to the top, what comes next is forming powerful—not popular—alliances with the right people. That means not just getting the most votes, or even any votes at any cost, but getting the right votes from the right people. In politics, the "right" votes are the electoral votes, the votes that really matter. In the workplace, the right votes are the powerful votes, the only votes that count.

The good news is that in the case of getting the right votes, less really *is* more. In fact, there are really only one or two votes that matter in your office. The bad news—or at least, the less-than-good news—is that getting the votes that matter isn't quite so easy as becoming Mr. or Ms. Popularity.

Who has the "electoral" votes in your office? Don't think popularity equals power, or even that power equals power. Some of the most powerful people in your office may be the least liked, the least effective, and even the least respected by the executives in the corner offices.

That's the danger of seeking the popular vote. We often think popularity equals power when, in fact, that isn't always true. To be sure, many powerful people are popular, but just as many aren't. So you can't always tell who is the most powerful simply by who is the most popular, yet many successful people make this same mistake all the time.

Remember, just because some people have a higher rank in the organization than you do, it doesn't necessarily mean that they are on their way to the top. Some so-called powerful people will never actually move from where they are; for whatever reason, they are trapped in time and going nowhere. Hitching your star to their wagon will only take you to the same place they're going: straight to mediocrity.

Maybe they don't respond well to pressure, maybe they're not socially adept, maybe they're crass or crude, or maybe they simply can't be trusted. It's easy when you're in a new position or have just joined a new team to get blinded by the status of someone above you, but before you form a fast allegiance with someone who you think is really on the fast track straight to the top, take a minute to stop, breathe, take a step back, and truly assess the situation.

Alliances can be good or bad, but a bad alliance can be nothing short of devastating. Cubicles are small, teams aren't much bigger, and even departments can feel small and insular from time to time; in short, nothing you do, say, or accomplish goes unnoticed.

The relationships you form are always suspect. If you choose the right alliance, it leads to bigger and better things; if you form the wrong alliance, it can stop you dead in your tracks.

The Two Levels of Workplace Relationships: Ally or Alliance

There are two additional terms you need on your rise to the top. The first term is "ally," someone you *want* to work with, a cubicle mate, a lunch buddy, someone to gossip with around the water cooler or maybe have a beer with after work. Your life will be filled with many allies over the course of your career. Some will be friends on and off the job, whereas others will just be people with whom you have a workplace friendship.

The second type of workplace relationship is an alliance. Alliances can be formed with people you *need* to form a closer bond with— people who not only can teach you things, improve your performance, show you the ropes, and teach by example but also can actually take you places.

Let's say you've just joined a company with the creative department. Your team consists of nine people: one supervisor, one manager, you, and six fellow creative types (editors, writers, copy editors, etc.). You spend a few months in the career management phase, learning the ropes, getting to know your team, mastering your job duties, turning in assignments, and so forth, and as you get a better handle on things you start to focus on job growth. So far, so good.

In the career management phase, you noticed, the team has two star players. Rudy is a supervisor, the big dog in charge. Maya is a manager, but unlike Rudy, who tends to focus on the big picture and not the smaller, day-to-day details, she's the one who *really* has her fingers on the pulse of the team. You realize that if you ever want to get promoted up the team ladder or removed from the team altogether and into a bigger, more influential department, you're going to have to form an alliance with one of these star players.

Who will you choose? If you're going by popular vote, Rudy is the obvious choice. Everyone likes him, he's a born leader, he dresses the part, and it sure seems like he makes a lot of money and is really going places. But take a closer look and really zero in on the details.

How long has he been in this same position? How much does he *really* make? Who is he really popular with? What is his work ethic? What can you point to that really indicates that he would be a powerful alliance? Where is his next step, that is, what is his next logical job choice and why hasn't he taken it yet? What do his superiors think of him? These are all vital questions to be asking yourself.

Now consider Maya. Maya may "only" be a manager, but in the short time you've been on her team, you can already tell she's the real brains behind the outfit. While Rudy is out wining and dining the creative clients, promising things he can't deliver, including deadlines no one in their right minds could meet, Maya stays behind and steers the ship—and always in the right direction.

She soothes management's nerves when clients call to complain, works late hours to meet unrealistic deadlines made by her boss (and without blaming him or causing a scene or quietly backstabbing or spreading rumors about him), is quick on her feet, and pays attention to details. The people in the corner office love her, and everyone who is anyone knows that it's just a matter of time before she makes her move and climbs to the top.

In this scenario, Rudy is likely someone you would want to consider an ally. In the politics of this particular team, it only makes sense to keep Rudy on your good side, make him happy when you can, and generally keep him as an ally. However, when you're looking to form a game-changing workplace alliance, Maya is clearly your first— and only—choice.

Trading Up!

When it comes to alliances, you always want to trade up. In other words, while you don't necessarily have to form an alliance with the highest-ranking person you know (witness Rudy versus Maya), you *always* want to form an alliance with someone in just a slightly better position than you.

It may be your manager or your supervisor. It may be someone who started in your position and is now in another department entirely. It may be someone who has a skill you'd like to master, like sales, technology, or networking. So don't go by rank alone; as you may have seen, some people in the middle to high ranks are stuck there and likely won't go any higher, so choosing based on position alone will only get you so far.

You need to learn how to predict who is going places. Maya, for example, simply has those innate qualities—dependability, attention to detail, personality, the ability to prioritize, and so on—that are valuable in any organization, in any department, and eventually, in any corner office or C-level position.

Just as interviewers, supervisors, recruiters, and HR departments must look past your external attributes to try and discover the internal X-Factor that makes you special, so you should look for the X-Factor in others. It's not always easy, but paying attention to detail—and not being blinded by the popular vote—will surely help.

Learn to look for these skills and adopt them in your own right. For instance, if you really respect the way a certain colleague handles himself or herself, let that colleague lead by example. Maybe he's a great team presenter who has learned to purge "uhhmms" and "you knows" from his vocabulary. Maybe she's just a genuine go-getter who has an amazing energy you'd like to duplicate for yourself. There's nothing wrong with asking someone outright, "How do you give such great presentations?" Or, "Where do you get your energy?"

Most people worthy of your respect are looking for a chance to share their expertise and are generally interested in helping others become the best they can be, so chances are they'd be more than happy to share their secrets. In this case, imitation really is the sincerest form of flattery.

I look at my success as a patchwork quilt of attributes, some of which were internal, that is, they came from my nature, my nurture, and all that I brought to the job in the first place. But many more pieces of my patchwork success have been those skills, attributes, tendencies, and outright influences I've learned from others while trading up to more and more success along the way.

In the same way that I have no problem sharing my success with others, I am equally solicitous of others and their success. If I see someone reading a new business book, I'll happily ask him or her who wrote it, what it's about, and is it any good. If someone really wows me with a presentation, a skill, or a habit, I will absolutely drill that person about it and "adopt" it as my own.

Not only will your talents evolve along the way with this winning strategy, but you will actively attract game-changers to you. Remember: like with like. People who work hard, work often, work smart, and work well within the team tend to flock together.

Remember back in school, when your teacher would put you in groups to give a presentation, conduct an experiment, or finish a report? Typically, in any group of four or five people, it's really only one or two who get the job done—fill in the blanks, organize the report, take the right measurements, do the research, and so on— while everybody else sits around, flaps their gums, and then takes collective credit.

In the workplace, those one or two active participants tend to find each other, work well together, and watch each other's backs. One of the best ways to form an alliance is simply to do those things that the people you want to work with do; then they'll want to work with you as well!

How to Choose Your Alliances:
10 Questions Every Employee Should Ask

Forming an alliance with someone at work is a very serious choice. After all, this is someone who can help your career, foster your growth, improve your performance, and generally change your game for the better. But before you form an alliance, ask yourself the following 10 questions to make sure you're choosing the right alliance, at the right time, with the right person:

1. *What is this person's reputation in the company?* Rank is one thing, and respect is another. Your reputation at work goes up when you form a powerful alliance; likewise, it goes down when you make the wrong choice. So watch and learn how this person is perceived in the company—you may be surprised what you learn when you do!

2. *Who is this person allied with?* An alliance is like a virus; you don't just align yourself with one person, but with every person that person is aligned with. So if your powerful friend has powerful friends, fantastic. You're in! But if your less-than-powerful friend has less-than-desirable affiliations, well, not so fantastic. Look out! Oftentimes, forming an alliance is a great thing, like joining an elusive and elite club. Other times, you can let the company you keep drag you down, if you're not careful to ask these kinds of questions first.

3. *What do his supervisors think of him?* Remember Rudy? Rudy was the supervisor of the creative department and he will probably always be the supervisor of the creative department. Why? Because his supervisors think he's a joke. On the other hand, everyone—from the bottom to the top of the company—who knows Maya respects her as a solid team player with a good head on her shoulders. So don't just see the person in a vacuum—see that person in relation to his or her supervisors, and their supervisors, and so on.

4. *How long has she been in this position?* If your manager has always been your manager—if she's always been a manager, period—chances are that may be her lot in life. And more power to her! But if you want more, if your goal truly is to play the game at the top, then you need to look beyond that person to align yourself with someone who can help you do more, get more, and possibly even *be* more.

3. *What are his odds of moving up?* Again, if the odds aren't good that the person you hope to align yourself with is going to move up anytime soon, chances are he or she can't help you move up either. It comes back to the philosophy of trading up where it's more than fine to have allies who will remain stationary, but if you're actively courting an alliance with someone you want to make sure this is someone who's on the same career trajectory as you are.

4. *What does your gut tell you about this person's ethics?* Instincts are very important on any job; it's no different when forming an alliance. Those things you can't see about a person, those things you have to trust your gut about because they are invisible to the naked eye, are often the most important things to notice. Listen to what your gut is saying. Not every employee on every job is going to be a saint, but, now more than ever, bad ethics are rarely rewarded. And even if they are, is that how *you* want to get the top?

5. *Would you work well together?* Bottom line, you can't form an alliance with a colleague if you don't work well together. Not every alliance is always going to be with your direct supervisor or in your department, but you *will* work for the same company and you want to make sure you align yourself with people you could see yourself working with, or even for, someday. It's often disappointing when someone who is otherwise perfect to form an alliance with drops out of the running simply because it's just very, very difficult to work with this person. But it's not really a mutual alliance if all 10 of these elements aren't present, so be very wary if you find it difficult to work with someone, even if nine other factors are all there.

6. *Would you feel comfortable asking this person to help you?* Playing at the top is not for the faint of heart; you do have to put

yourself out there, stretch your skills, and take chances. Are you comfortable with the idea of forming an alliance with this person? If so, it's probably a good idea. If not, then ask yourself, "Why am I hesitating to make this alliance? What about this person is giving me second thoughts?" Remember how powerful your gut instinct can be, and before you trust someone else or the power they may or may not possess, always trust your instincts first.

7. *Do you really think this person* can *help you?* In some cases, the most popular people at work are simply that: popular. They're not powerful, they hold no real value for you, and they're basically just blowing smoke if they tell you they can get you x, y, or z. Those who can't really help themselves are not in a good position to help you either.

8. *What, specifically, makes you want to form an alliance with this person?* If you can't pinpoint, specifically and quickly (or even immediately), why you want to be associated with this person—for instance, he has great contacts, she is very detail oriented, he knows his stuff, she's going places—he or she likely won't make a good alliance. People who immediately strike you for one reason or another—dynamic, expert, well-educated, go-getter, dependable, and so on—are the kind about whom you can clearly say, "*This* is why I want to form an alliance." If you can't get excited about working with a person, chances are nobody else can either.

Why Forging the Right Alliance Is Priceless, and Forging the Wrong Alliance Is Deadly

No matter how many people work at your company, it only takes one or two people to significantly change the game you're playing. Choosing whom to align yourself with on the job will make all the difference. Forging alliances in the workplace is a lot like getting elected: it's not who's the most popular who wins, but who has proven himself or herself to be the most influential with the right people who ultimately gets the top spot.

If you don't do your research, if you're not vigilant about who you're courting and what your alliance's role is in the company itself, you could wind up aligning yourself with someone who is not very popular in the higher echelon, or even someone who might be on the way out of employment with the company (and not by choice).

Remember: Such negative associations can do more harm than good.

Action Plan for Forming the Right Alliances

As you have seen by now, there are two types of alliances: popular and powerful. The popular alliance, of course, has its obvious drawbacks, and the powerful alliance has its obvious benefits.

What's important for you to do now is to identify which kind of alliance is which. In the spaces listed below, list every alliance you've formed at work to date.

Don't worry about categorizing them all just yet; we'll get to all that. For now I just want you to list every alliance so they're immediately available to you as you begin to categorize them later in this exercise:

_____

_____

_____

_____

_____

_____

_____

_____

_____

Now, in the next section, using the list you just generated, write down only the names of those people who fall into the popular category:

_____

_____

_____

_____

_____

Finally, in the spaces below, list only those people who are powerful, who represent the kinds of alliances you want to form, nurture, and capitalize on as you scratch your way to the top:

_____

_____

_____

You can see that the lists contain fewer and fewer blanks each time; that's because you're filtering the list down to only the most vital and important people. Much as you've narrowed down your list of alliances from popular to powerful, I want you to filter your relationships at work. It doesn't mean you can't still be funny, happy, and popular, but just don't put all your eggs in that one basket.

Know who can help you and who can't. More importantly, know where to put the bulk of your energies when it comes to forming alliances. If you would like help filtering this list and identifying your electoral vote list and how to leverage it, visit www.corporateclimb. net.

Rule #6

Managing Your Peers and Keeping Your "Enemies" Close

IN EVERY POSITION YOU WILL HAVE PEERS—COWORKERS, colleagues, and allies who are on the same basic employment level with you and who can either hurt or help your career. Although it may sound mercenary, it's important to think of them this way: who can hurt and who can help?

You don't have to be so blatant about it that you keep a running scorecard on every employee in every division (who's been naughty and who's been nice); just get yourself in the mindset of always thinking along these lines.

Often, people will approach you as a peer only to later become an enemy. Who knows why they turn on you? Employee relationships often remain a mystery to me, even though I've been in the corporate landscape for decades now.

Likewise, just because someone acts like an enemy doesn't mean he or she is not a peer. Let's face it, some people are inherently competitive and not very nice. It's important in these instances to look beyond the superficial to make informed decisions on more than just first impressions.

Why is it important to manage your peers? And why is it imperative for you to really understand who your enemies are? And why would you want to keep your enemies closer to you? In this chapter, I'll talk about how to interact with your peers so that you can avoid seeing them turn into enemies—and what to do if all else fails.

Peers Versus Enemies: The Critical Difference

Peers are those people you eat lunch with and hang out with after work and who share your common story: entry level when you're entry level, single when you're single, hungry for more when you're hungry, promoted when you're promoted. More than age or income, they share a common workplace bond with you.

Peers are there in the trenches, working overtime with you, getting there early, or slacking off as stress demands. Peers are often mirror images of you, reflecting back truths about yourself.

Enemies are out to get you, plain and simple. I'm not going to sugarcoat it because these are definitely people you want to avoid. Who knows why they're out to get you. It may be personal, or it may be professional, but what makes an enemy an enemy is that person's singular goal to see harm come your way. You don't run into them as often as peers (thank goodness), but there is always the potential that a peer will turn into an enemy so you *do* have to be careful. After all, prevention is often the key to avoidance, so the more you do to be proactive about avoiding enemies in the first place, the fewer enemies you could cultivate while you're at the company in question.

The good thing about enemies—possibly the *only* good thing about enemies—is that while they themselves may be cagey, mysterious, and cryptic, what they want from you is not. They want you gone—or, if not gone altogether, at least diminished in some capacity, demoted, or paralyzed with no promotions.

It's rare to find an enemy with no ties to your department, division or career path. Typically, an enemy is someone in direct competition with you, hence the more that person can do to squash your career, the better he or she looks in comparison.

It is sad that although the emphasis throughout this book has been on helping others, the reality is that some (many) people are merely out for themselves. But it's better to know the truth ahead of time than to be surprised when you come face to face with it in the workplace.

When Peers Attack: How Will You React?

If you think about it realistically, even when you get along great with your peers, if you're someone who is trying to advance and grow your career and get promoted to the next level, you're actually competing with them.

Particularly with entry-level employees, there are always more than enough candidates for one or two departmental promotions. In other words, they're not going to promote the whole secretarial pool! One will move up, and the others will stay behind. That's just the nature of the beast. Some people, unfortunately, are so insecure about their own job skills that rather than face competition fairly by accepting that promotions are based on performance or productivity, they prefer to hamstring the competition by making them look as bad as possible; this includes making you look bad in the process.

So if you and your peers are following the same type of career paths—you start low and aim high—eventually you will be in direct competition with each other. Maybe it will be to see who does the best on an ad campaign, who can increase productivity by 2 percent next quarter, or who will get your manager's job when he or she leaves next month. Either way, competition can put stress on any relationship, particularly those in the workplace.

As a result of this constant battle for the top, peers will occasionally become your enemies. Whatever their dirty tactics might be, however nasty they start to fight, you have to stay beyond reproach.

So when a peer relationship goes sour and someone you once trusted is now out to sabotage your performance, promotion, or entire career, you can't fight fire with fire—you can't stoop to that person's level. As hard as it sounds, and as even harder as it will be to do in real life, you have to take the high road.

Let's say you and Jeremy started your job in the accounting department at pretty much the same time. As the two newest candidates on a team of six, it only made sense that you would "buddy up" and learn the ropes together. But you learned more than that; as a result of your close work relationship, maybe you and Jeremy drifted into an off-site friendship as well. You hung out, played sports together, met each other's significant other. Or, if the relationship didn't move off-site, your work relationship was such that Jeremy knew who you liked in the department, who you didn't, who you'd gossip about, what you thought of your boss, and so on.

Can you see how quickly a peer relationship can disintegrate when you are both up for a promotion? Can you see how easy it would be for Jeremy to use his inside information on you—or simply to invent information out of thin air—for his own gain? How easy would it be for Jeremy to talk about your drinking habits, your dating habits, your debt load, your car payments, your housing situation—any number of personal facts about you that you'd rather be kept private—simply because of his personal access to you during off hours?

I'm not saying you can't trust anyone at work—what a dismal and paranoid life *that* would be! What I *am* saying is to remember where you are, to act professionally, and to avoid the kind of interoffice gossip, innuendo, and slander that would give a peer-turned-enemy like Jeremy ammunition if your relationship was to go south.

That's why taking the high road is so appropriate in these situations. When you are above reproach, guys like Jeremy have no ammunition because, based on your spotless reputation, few in the workplace would believe you would do such things in the first place.

So where does Jeremy go from there? He can't ding you with slander because no one believes it; hence, he has no leverage so he moves on to another workplace enemy, but by then he's the boy who cried wolf, and nobody believes him anyway.

Understand the Span of Control

Most corporate executives have what is called a span of control. A span of control encompasses the people you are managing on your team or in your department. In other words, how many employees are you controlling? A typical span of control is about eight to 11 employees; that means fewer than a dozen direct reports for each manager, supervisor, or team leader.

Consider the wait-staff system in a restaurant. Every day, the servers come in and are assigned their span of control; that is, how many tables they'll be waiting on that day. A low span of control is one or two tables, and the wait staff is not going to make any money that way. A high span of control is maybe seven or eight tables—that's a lot to handle and when the floor gets busy during lunch or dinner, things are going to get hectic; the server could lose out on tips because of the reduced service.

So usually servers manage about four to six tables a shift, depending on the restaurant, the menu, the clientele, the server, and so on. Corporate America isn't that different from your average restaurant; you don't want too few or too many employees, so more than half a dozen and fewer than a dozen works to keep the span of control reasonable for any self-respecting supervisor.

Among those eight to eleven direct reports are people who are just as inspired or determined and focused as you are to maybe one day step into your leadership position. Maybe they are even *more* determined and focused to achieve another level of promotion that may be beyond your leadership position and put themselves in your supervisor's spot.

So, in essence, even though they are technically "under" you, you are competing with those eight to eleven direct reports to your boss.

You really need to understand that—this is not a joke. But it's also important that you appreciate the fact that you're not trying to make your peers look bad or do things that would make them look bad or put them on the spot, because that's not a professional thing to do.

However, some people coming into corporate America misconstrue that their competition is actually outside the company when, in fact, you are always competing both externally and internally. So in a very real sense, it's not just external companies that you're competing with. You're actually competing internally if you're a person who is trying to grow your career. (And who isn't?)

Take the High Road (Straight to the Top)

So, as noted, in your career, there are some peers who will become enemies. How do you deal with those peers? In my career, I've had peers who've turned into enemies on me. And one of the things that I wanted to do is not to react at all. I didn't want to react in a way that would put me in a worse position. Remember, enemies want you to react; they expect you to react.

Have you ever heard the phrase, "Never let your enemies see you sweat"?

When you don't react, when you continue to work hard and do your job, when you, in fact, "kill them with kindness," that simply leaves enemies with nowhere to go. The worst thing you can do in any workplace enemy situation is respond exactly the way they want you to respond.

Even when you feel like going after enemies, retaliating, defending yourself, having a tantrum, or breaking a computer monitor over their head, think of the consequences; better yet, think of the satisfaction you'll get by denying that workplace enemy the reaction he or she desires most.

When someone attacks you, spreads a rumor, puts you down, betrays you, or lies behind your back, it's only natural that you will immediately and reflexively want to react to that. But stop to think about this for a moment: When you take that fire and pour gasoline on it by overreacting, threatening, freaking out, disputing everything, and so forth, how do you then look to the people who *really* matter?

It's easy to focus on your enemy at this point, but he or she does *not* matter. Even though being threatened, targeted, and singled out for abuse makes you preoccupied with the abuser, don't lose sight of the big picture: again, this person doesn't matter. This person can't help you; this person can only hurt you.

Who *can* help you right now? The only people who matter: supervisors, colleagues, higher-ups, mentors, and so on. Those people, not the powerless person trying to drag you down, are who you should be thinking of now. When you help that person fan the flames, when you overreact and freak out, you are helping him or her take you down.

No matter what was going on around me in the workplace—good, bad, or indifferent—I never wanted to be in a position where I wasn't looking the best that I could look. I was always considering the following questions:

- How am I carrying myself right now?
- How am I presenting myself?
- How am I being perceived at this very moment?
- Are my actions helping my case?
- Are my actions hurting my case?
- Am I acting maturely, professionally, calmly, and rationally?
- Am I putting myself in a position where I can hurt myself for any advancement for future opportunities by taking it out on this enemy right now?

If you are ever in a situation where your peer has done something to betray you, and you're just livid about what he or she has done and you want to react, the reality is that it's usually the people who react, who get caught up in the drama, and who are not remembered for their good behavior—they are remembered only for their bad. And so you never, ever want to be seduced into bad behavior.

It's unfortunate that others can try to drag you down with them; it's even more unfortunate when you help them succeed. Have you ever heard the term "guilt by association"? The fact is that when someone is behaving badly and you join him or her, regardless of whether you were the victim in this case, you will only be remembered for your bad behavior.

In fact, some enemies will purposefully dupe you into reacting badly; when you do, you only give them more ammunition. One of my mentors once told me, "Kill your enemies with kindness." By that, she meant that when someone is doing you harm, he actively wants you to blow up, freak out, and threaten so he can run to your supervisor and say, "See, what'd I tell you? The guy is unstable! Listen to how loud he's getting! Look at how red his face is!"

When you kill them with kindness, though, when you redouble your efforts and act even more professionally, they have nowhere to go with that. You take the wind out of their sails.

I've coached and mentored people about this very topic throughout my career. Remember, no matter how tempting it may be, you simply can't let someone else's behavior put you in a position where your behavior is highlighted and spotted and is seen in turn as bad behavior. All it achieves is stopping you from achieving your goals.

So you always have to remain calm, cool, and collected. You have to begin to process how you want to respond to this particular person who has no intentions of seeing you become successful. It seems strange that someone who is on your team, who is a peer, and who is in the trenches with you wouldn't want you to succeed, especially when you naturally want that person to succeed, when you only want everyone to win.

However, people who are trying to stop you from getting to the top of your game are out there. Most of the time, unfortunately, they're not strangers—they're your peers.

Keep Your Enemies Close

One of the things I've practiced in my career that I would ask you to do and to think about in your climb to the top is keeping your enemies close. It's important that, once you find out who's against you, you do not push them away.

Instead, you really have to understand that they're there and they're not going away anytime soon. How do you deal with them? Particularly when your ultimate goal is to become a consummate executive, you want a two-pronged strategy:

1. First, you want your enemies to know that you know they're out to do you harm. Just because you're not going to throw a tantrum and scream and cry and shout, that doesn't mean you have to let enemies get away with anything either. In fact, one of the most effective methods for dealing with workplace enemies is letting them know you know they're your enemy—and still reacting professionally.

2. Second, you want to make sure that they are closer to you than ever before. It's human nature to want to avoid confrontation, to want to run from a fight, or even to stick our heads in the sand and forget the problem exists altogether. But in this case, I recommend that rather than run or hide from your enemy, you turn the tables and keep him or her closer than ever.

You *really* want to make sure your enemies know that you know they have no intentions of seeing you become successful. Turn the tables so that their intentions are not only out in the open but impotent. You do that by inviting them into your staff meetings, by bringing them into the light, and by forcing them—and their intentions—out into the open. In other words, you keep your enemies closer than ever to make sure everyone knows who they are, what they're doing, and, more importantly, how you're reacting.

So if you're head of a supply chain, for example, and one of your enemies is running the sales portion of your boss's group, you invite your enemy to your supply-chain staff meeting or supply-chain annual meeting and have your enemy lecture about what she's doing from a sales perspective.

Have her talk about what she plans on doing to grow the sales business and how much supply your business or your group can expect to see. This way, since others are there, she has to pony up the details and reveal her plans. And, as I've noted numerous times throughout this book, knowledge is power. The more you know about your enemy and her plans, the less power she has—and the more power you have.

Next, get her to talk about how her department's negotiating contracts with original design manufacturers to improve the products and their efficiency. Put her on the spot. Make her perform. The bottom line is you want to make sure that you're keeping your enemy close to you to disclose what she is up to.

The biggest impact that you get from this strategy is that now *you're* being perceived as the one who's working with your enemy, even though other people in the company know she's trying to do you harm (and they always seem to know).

Perception in these situations is key. You can't let this enemy derail your career plans. Instead, you have to turn your enemy's plans for you around and use them to your advantage. By keeping your enemy close and acting in a professional manner, you take that person's power away and come out looking better in the bargain.

In this way, you are being a consummate executive. You are remaining above reproach because you are the one who is reaching out to someone who you know has no good intentions about your success.

More importantly, the employees in your group *know* that you're reaching out to your enemy, and you're setting a great example from a leadership perspective. Finally, by ensuring that the people who have no good intentions about your success are kept as close to you as possible, you retain the ability to understand what they're doing.

Leverage Your Enemies

The important thing to remember when you find yourself with an enemy at work is that you are not alone. Specifically, leadership should be aware of the friction between you and this other employee and be able to do something about it, or at least help *you* to do something about it.

If you have a good leader, he or she is already tuned into some of the friction on this team. And that leader—who's in the position to promote you to the next level, to his or her job, or to recommend that you get promoted outside of your function to a job that's outside of his or her responsibility—will take into consideration how you manage your peers.

All good leaders know that management is a critical job skill in every department. They also know that it's easy to manage the peers you get along with. It's really, really hard to successfully manage peers you don't get along with. To leaders, that's the true test.

An executive who tells you that he or she has never had any fallouts with peers is an unsuccessful executive. You have to master the art of managing your peers, and one way to do that is to not shut any doors on your enemies.

You want to keep the lines of communication open and clear, and you want to be transparent. That's how you leverage your peer to get you the success that you want and that you worked so hard to achieve.

Action Plan for Keeping Your Enemies Close

Do you know who your enemies are? It's important that you aren't caught unawares by unsuspected enemies at work, particularly after reading in this chapter about the damage they can do.

In the previous Action Plan, you listed all the powerful and popular people in your company. Now with this Action Plan, you're going to list the people you most feel threatened by, who can do you—and your career—the most harm and who might derail your trip to the top rather than help it along.

In the lines below, write down the names of those people who you consider enemies or potential enemies:

_____

_____

_____

_____

_____

Next, in the following spaces, whittle the list you just created to a more manageable—and likely more realistic—depiction of who in your office, team, department, or company poses the most significant threat to your career:

_____

_____

_____

Time is important when labeling enemies. To ensure that you don't waste inordinate amounts of time keeping track on all of your enemies, real or perceived, use the narrowing-down lists on the previous page to determine your single most dangerous enemy and list him or her below:

_____

Rule #7

Green—The Only Color They See!

LET ME TELL YOU A LITTLE SECRET ABOUT PLAYING AT the top that most other business books won't share with you. Your boss may talk about inspiration, your manager may fill you with purpose, your coworkers may be passionate, your HR rep may encourage you to take classes to perfect your art, and you may have read every best-selling business book ever written—but at the end of the day, "the only color they see is green."

In other words, money is the end all and the be all, the alpha and the omega, the beginning and the end. You can have your MBA, your Ivy League degree, your three-piece suit, your "Success" wall posters, and the popular vote of every single one of your coworkers—*but* if you're not producing, if you're not performing, if you are not every day helping the company to succeed, move forward, win, innovate, and make money, the top of the game will always be just out of reach.

It doesn't matter what department you're in; that department exists to help the company win and make money. For example, the advertising department is expected to get results. Those results are measured in increased sales, which translates to actual dollars.

So if you are in advertising, yes, absolutely, it helps to be creative, intelligent, well-educated, innovative, and clever, but not for the sake of simply being creative, intelligent, well-educated, innovative, and clever. Your boss needs you to use those particular talents to get results, that is, increase business through those traits.

The sales department is expected to produce. How does leadership benchmark those results? In sales numbers, which translate to new clients, orders, or business. So your success is closely monitored not in how popular you are, not in how many sports stats you can reel off at the drop of the hat, and not with how often you smile, but with how often you produce results, rack up sales, and help the company win and make money.

In this chapter, expect to learn the rarely discussed, bottom-line truth about business: it's about winning and making money. You'll also understand how to assess your impact.

In other words, how efficient are you with your resources? How do you leverage your resources? I will also help you understand how to tailor your services by offering to be the best among the competition and helping to position your company for growth outside of the U.S. Finally, you will learn what I did to get noticed and to position myself for success from a financial perspective.

The Company Can't Love You Back

It's not something we think about every day when we walk into work, but if you've ever wondered why businesses exist, the answer is simple: to make money.

Yes, they may give back to their community, contribute to local charities, recycle 35 percent of their waste products, match your 401(k) program, and offer retirement benefits, but how much of all that do you think they could do—or even *would* do—if they stopped making money tomorrow?

It's becoming increasingly clear that American corporations care only about the bottom line. Gone are many corporate perks of yesterday, the outside consultants giving day-long workshops on creativity and idea generation in the conference room, the travel allowances, the gift baskets, the Cheer Club budget, and any and all other places where they could slash the budget to create more profits.

Meanwhile, employees are expected to work harder and longer hours for the same or even less benefits—for example, a demotion, a reduction in pay, flat-line raises, or lower bonuses.

My mentor had a saying that always put things in perspective for me. He said, "Never love the company, because the company can't love you back." To me that means never get so caught up in thinking, "Wow, I love this company. I'm willing to do everything that I can for this company."

Don't get me wrong—that certainly *is* a good feeling to have. However, some people get so caught up in this feeling of partnership and togetherness that they don't realize that the company is always going to do what's best for the company.

In short, the company can't love you back because there is simply no profit in it.

There have been people, especially in these tough economic times, who have worked for corporations for years, decades even. Some employees have worked for a company for 10, 15, 20, or 25 years, have never missed a day of work, always talked up the company, gave their all, and never in a million years thought that a representative of the corporation would knock on their door and say, "Look, we don't need your services anymore," or, "Listen, we're outsourcing your services to overseas."

And yet, there they are, out on the street. Why? Probably because the ones who have been the most loyal and who have been the most productive earn the most. Hence, they have the biggest salaries and the more of those employees the company can cut, the less they have to pay out in payroll and benefits every month.

I've also heard the idea that the job of the corporation is to pay you just enough so that you won't leave. The goal isn't to make you wealthy or help you get ahead—it is a transaction, a trade, and nothing else.

You have to put things in perspective. Work hard, produce, perform, enjoy your coworkers, decorate your cubicle, stay as long as you're welcome, be fond of the company—but never *love* the company, because the company can't love you back.

My First Green Experience

When most companies talk about "going green," it means they're introducing a new product line that is good for the environment. But would they be doing that if it weren't good for the company?

When I say that you should work on your "green experience," I'm referring to how your performance enhances the company's financial experience or how you are helping the company make money (green).

One of my first jobs in sales was working for one of the biggest transportation companies in the world. I took on a role as a sales executive in a region that wasn't very popular at the time: Chicago. Big city transportation is a very tough, grinding industry. However, from a financial and a profitability perspective, it can also be a very lucrative industry. If you run your operations right, you can make a lot of money in transportation.

Although my business card read "sales executive," I was not sitting in some corner office running the empire from on high; this was a street-level, down-and-dirty job. And while Chicago's skyline, four-star restaurants, and top-notch hotels are certainly glamorous, my sales area was one of the toughest in Chicago.

I had to go into areas that were known as gang turf and where gangs operated to make many of my sales calls. I considered this to be a personal and professional challenge, because even then I knew that success is not achieved without hard, challenging work. (And success certainly isn't achieved overnight.)

Despite the challenges I faced in this area of sales, I was able to flourish through persistence and hard work. In fact, in the five years I was with this company, I grew this area from about $200,000 in revenue a month to more than $6 million a month.

That accomplishment led me to receive the Sales Executive of the Year award within my region four out of the five years I worked for this company. By anyone's standards, even mine, that was a huge and significant accomplishment.

Those five years were very formative for me because, during this time, I began to think about such hard-charging, career-growth–oriented questions, such as, "Where do I want to go beyond sales? What other things do I need to do to enhance my career?" I realized that if I was going to branch out from being a sales executive to becoming a consummate executive, at some point, I probably needed to continue my education.

So, as I achieved success from a sales perspective and broke record numbers and received all kinds of sales awards from my success, I also ended up getting my master's degree. And the company paid for it! But after I had received my master's degree, it was clear to me that I needed to move on. I decided that I wanted to do something that I was passionate about, and fortunately, my graduate degree was in a discipline that I was passionate about: organizational development.

As I noted when speaking of my own X-Factor, organizational development is something that I believe I would do even if I didn't get paid one penny. It's something that I wake up every morning inspired to do. Organizational development (OD) is a function that allows me to touch every aspect of a corporation: I am involved with sales, marketing, finance, customer service, supply chain, and so on.

When you're the OD leader, your job is to figure out how to make all those departments function as efficiently and as effectively as they can and to ensure that the strategies that have been laid out by the senior leader of that company are indeed executed from a talent perspective.

In other words, often it is the OD leader's role to tell a senior executive how to help his or her department perform better so that the company can win and make money. If you're working to get to the top, there's no better job to be in.

Assess Your Impact on the Bottom Line

Success is about impact. What is your impact on the company's bottom line? How are you helping the company win? How, specifically, are you making the organization money or, at least, helping the organization to make money?

Your impact on a company is defined in black and white. There are no fuzzy gray areas or philosophical arguments—either you're specifically helping the company make money, or you're costing them money (by getting paid and not making much of an impact).

Consider sales, for instance: either you hit the number you needed to hit that day, week, month, or quarter, or your didn't. It's not about who's the most popular, looks the best, drives the flashiest car or has the biggest expense account—either you hit the number or your didn't. This is known as a green result, and green results transcend all of the other workplace distractions, including the crazy little things people may do to try to stop you from achieving success, as discussed in the previous chapter.

So maybe a peer starts a rumor about the state of your marriage, maybe someone tries to demean you in the morning staff meeting, or maybe someone trashes your reputation or calls your wardrobe into question. These are petty results, results that don't matter.

Only green results matter. In many cases, from day to day, that's all your boss wants to know about—not what car you drove to work that morning, not the color of your tie, and not if you're married, single, gay, or straight, but did you hit your numbers? If you got your green results, well, if it's important, the rest can all be sorted out later. Keep getting results, and little else matters.

I was fortunate enough to get green results, even when I was competing with people who had been in the industry for 5, 10, or 15 years longer than I had been at the time. These people were very well equipped and knowledgeable about the transportation industry, yet their results weren't as green as mine. My returns mattered to the executives who mattered, and as a result, they propelled me to the top of that particular industry—and beyond. It doesn't matter what your graduate degree is in, where you got it, how long you've been working in the field, or, for that matter, how old you are; the bottom line is now, always was, and forever will be results.

So You're Not in Sales

You may be wondering how you assess your impact if you're *not* in sales. One of the things I've noted throughout this book is that it's not just the immediate results in a ledger that count. Sales numbers are merely the results by which salespeople, not *all* people, are measured. If you're not in sales, you still measure your impact by setting specific goals and objectives that you hope to attain, often on a daily, weekly, monthly, or at least regular basis. While goals and objectives may sound esoteric, the more specific the goals and objectives are, the more measurable they are.

Most well-run companies have the ability to set goals that are aligned with the business's overall financial objectives. For instance, if you work in the creative department, your supervisor might set a goal that states, "Employee X will generate ads that increase revenue by 5 percent this quarter." That is a measurable—and highly achievable— goal because you can compare revenue from last quarter to this quarter and measure that quantitatively. So you, as the individual contributor, can see your performance and understand with what your results are being compared.

In other words, did you generate ads that increased revenue by 5 percent this quarter? Or did your ads increase revenue by 10 percent? Or only 1 percent? Either way, you are able to tell at a glance whether your goal was met or not.

Most companies have some sort of performance management process in place for reviewing employees at least three times a year. First, there is an initial meeting where you set your goals and objectives. Next, there is a mid-year review to check your status in meeting those objectives. Finally, by the end of the year, you either know if you hit those goals and objectives or you didn't.

Even if you're not in sales, you can still check your performance as it relates to various benchmarks, goals, and objectives throughout these regular performance checkups. These checkups will measure your impact and its effect on the company's bottom-line profits.

What Is Your Green Initiative?

Remember that there are multiple ways of making money for your company and helping your company win. Some green results are easier to see than others, but results are results, and if you can measure them, you can grow them. And the more you grow as an employee, the more tools you acquire throughout your career, and the more resources you leverage, the more valuable you become not just for your company but also for *any* company.

Throughout my career, I've been able to grow from a personal development and educational perspective. Some employees are so caught up with and focused on making money that they forget to take advantage of some of the tools and instruments that corporations have in place to help them directly affect their green results.

For instance, if you analyze the statistics for companies that offer tuition reimbursement for advanced degree programs, you might be amazed by how few employees take advantage of the opportunity.

One of the things I leveraged early in my career was for my employer to pay for my master's degree, because the company offered tuition reimbursement. The company wanted to foster learning and development, and taking advantage of that program, in turn, helped give me options.

As you grow your career, you want to create options for yourself. I could have certainly stayed in the transportation industry and become a vice president. But I ruled out doing that because there were some things about the industry that I didn't like. However, I leveraged some of the tools that the corporation had to create options for me beyond getting that paycheck, beyond getting big bonuses and other benefits I was receiving and was naturally quite happy with.

I encourage you to understand the tools that are available to you beyond pay and benefits. What other tools, from a development and group perspective, does the company have that you can leverage, that will create options for you internally and externally?

Do You Know How to Beat the Competition?

People often talk about becoming the best, but do we know what that *really* means? Defining your goals and objectives becomes extremely important as you grow your career, and failing to do so can often cost you and your company what you both appreciate: winning and making more money.

As you think about tailoring your service offerings to be the best among the competition, you've got to first understand what the best is. Ask yourself what you are measuring to be considered the best? How are other industries considering or measuring what is the best?

For me and the companies that I've been a part of, the gold standard has always been this: Are you making money and are you the best at what you do among your competition? We often think we are the best judge to assess what is best for us, for the company, and for our career. But, in fact, the judge is the consumer. Are the consumers buying your products? Are the consumers looking at you as a trendsetter or a trend follower? You can get reports to figure out if you're actually leading in your area of expertise regarding the products and services that you're offering. Remember that results are key to your "green impact," and they come in the form of increased business, not just your increased confidence.

Innovation Lessons from GCI and Apple

In today's competitive landscape, beating your competition is tough because everyone is after you. People say that once you're at the top, there's nowhere to go but down, and they're actually right. After all, if you're number one, you have a bull's-eye painted on your back; suddenly you're the target, the best, the one to beat. However, to beat and stay ahead of your competition, I believe innovation is the solution.

I started a company called Global Consumer Innovation, Inc. (GCI; www.globalconsumerinnovation.com). One of the reasons I started this company was to help corporations figure out how to manage and grow their businesses at the same time and create a revenue stream beyond their imagination.

Consider what happened at Apple. Today Apple might be the gold standard in modern technology, but as recently as five or six years ago, Apple was on the verge of being split up, if not going out of business entirely. However, the company innovated its way into being the cool, sexy leader in desktops and producing the very sleekest of portable devices.

But Apple didn't just turn itself around—the company created phenomena that revolutionized modern technology, including the iPod and iTunes. That's innovation. It allowed Apple to create new revenue streams that it didn't have in its organization, which propelled the company not only to success but also well beyond its closest competition.

But it wasn't easy—it was a disruption. How so? It disrupted the status quo; Apple had to stop doing certain things, reroute funds, and go back to the drawing board to create these new technologies that helped propel the company past its competitors. That disruption lasted through some pretty tough times, and there was no guarantee of what awaited the company on the other end.

Of course, now everyone is trying to follow Apple's lead via duplication or imitation. The company's ability to innovate through disruption is the reason Apple is perceived as number one in its industry. At GCI, the focus is on challenging corporations to figure out how to grow their business beyond the current set of products. We strongly believe that you have to do that through disruptive innovation.

Grow Your Career Through Innovation

I can imagine that you are thinking, "That's all well and good for a company like Apple, but what does this really mean for me, as an individual working for a corporation?" And you're absolutely right.

Most people will not be in a position to have the type of innovation impact that I'm talking about. But what you should understand from this section is how, from an innovation perspective, you can leverage disruptive innovation to create opportunities for yourself.

If you're a new MBA grad and you're entering corporate America, or you're someone who is already in corporate America and you're trying to figure out how to grow your career, stop and think about what you can do differently to innovate yourself and your performance to produce green results for the company.

Consider how your job has been done in the past, and then think about how can you go to your boss and then prove, from efficiency and effectiveness perspectives, what you're doing that will allow the company to be much more productive than it's ever been in the past.

I've seen employees who have taken those types of initiatives and succeeded beyond their wildest dreams. This strategy has two specific benefits:

1. First, it sends a strong message to your boss that you have the capacity to do more than what you've been asked to do, that you're ready to make a greater green impact than what they expect of you.

2. Second, it shows that you're creative. It shows your leadership capability—that you're about helping the company win, that you're not just complacent about the status quo, and that you're thinking about how you can help this company grow and win.

The challenge is to meet expectations, then exceed them. So first you have to do your job at an acceptable level, then do it better. How can you do this? You need to assess your day-to-day duties from an entirely new perspective, such as how you might save time here or be more efficient there. Oftentimes exceeding expectations isn't as difficult as you might think if you simply analyze the process you're engaged in now, one step at a time.

Action Plan for Innovation

Here is a simple questionnaire you can use to help create more
innovation in any job you do. First read the questionnaire, then use
the blank template to fill in your answers to help you determine how
you can build innovation around every work skill:

1. *How am I using this particular skill today?* Let's say you want
   to cut down on the amount of time you spend reading,
   answering, deleting, and sorting your e-mail every day. First,
   assess how you're doing this skill today. Do you check your
   e-mail every five minutes? Do you have it on alert so that
   every time a "bleep" sounds, you look up from what you're
   doing and check it?

2. *How can I use this particular skill differently tomorrow?* Now,
   think of how you can check your e-mail differently tomorrow.
   Maybe only check it once an hour, or maybe check it every 15
   minutes instead of every five minutes. Consider prioritizing
   e-mails quickly, answering only work-related e-mails first and
   saving less important ones for later.

3. *Which method would work best for innovating this skill?* Of
   the various methods you've considered to solve your e-mail
   problems, list them in the order you think will work best.
   Maybe your list will look like this: "(1) check e-mail every 15
   minutes, (2) check once an hour, (3) flag important e-mails, and
   file the rest." This list will be helpful in systematically changing
   how you approach e-mail from a different perspective.

4. *Did it work or not?* Now, from among the ways you considered
   innovating your routine for e-mail, pick one and try it the
   next day. Let's say you decided to check your e-mail every 15
   minutes instead of every five minutes. Was that more efficient
   for you? Or, did you end up spending more time on e-mail
   because so many had accumulated?

5.   *What alternative might work better?* The potential for one idea to not work is why you made a list, prioritized it, and left yourself alternatives. If the first method on your list doesn't work, try the next one; if that doesn't work, try the one after that.

Now, here's the same list for you to fill in yourself:

1. How am I using this particular skill today?

_____

_____

_____

_____

2. How can I use this particular skill differently tomorrow?

_____

_____

_____

_____

3. Which method would work best for innovating this skill?

_____

_____

_____

4. Did it work or not?

_____

_____

_____

_____

5. What alternative might work better?

_____

_____

_____

_____

Rule #8

Corporate Winning

WINNING AT THE CORPORATE LEVEL IS ACHIEVED through a series of (mostly, until now) unwritten rules that have an impact on things far beyond performance and profits. Although both are the driving force behind your success, neither is quite enough by itself.

For instance, if you're a misogynist brute who sexually harasses his assistants and is regularly putting the company's legal department on notice about yet another complaint, regardless of your performance, you'll never get to the top, even if you *do* manage to keep your job through the next quarter.

Likewise, your sales numbers may be through the roof, but if you can't be bothered to take a shower, groom yourself, or use deodorant, there's a limit to how many clients are going to put up with that during your regular sales calls.

In other words, performance matters, but so does your personal hygiene, personality, style, and grace. These are the unwritten barometers by which a consummate corporate executive is measured, and to ignore them is to do so at your own peril.

It All Begins with Etiquette and Style

Etiquette is more than just walking with your back straight and your head up; it is more than matching solids with stripes and tans with browns. The new winning business etiquette is about the whole package—your manners, your attitude, and how well you listen.

Consummate corporate executives have a certain way about them. I know because not only have I been one but I've also worked and associated with them for most of my career. You can tell when someone stands out or doesn't belong or when someone is coarse, brash, rude, and a bad listener.

These things may sound like personal traits that shouldn't have anything to do with your career, but in a capitalist society, what matters to your superiors is really all that matters. As has been reiterated throughout this book, most corporate executives want to put like with like; they want to evoke a certain sense of etiquette and style—not just in-house but for socializing with clients, newspaper editors, reporters, or prospects.

So the new winning business etiquette is about style, substance, and sophistication and how all of these things play into your role and your ability to move your career forward.

Listen with the Intent to Hear

Listening may not be the first thing you think of when you hear the word "etiquette," but how you listen, respond, and interact with people in both personal and professional situations says a lot about your manners.

Listening is a particularly critical business skill. Many people think they are absolutely fantastic listeners, but unfortunately, a lot of people listen with the intent to speak as opposed to listening with the intent to hear. People who listen with the intent to speak do not actually hear what the individual is saying. Rather, they are already thinking about what they're going to say in response that will make them sound better than the person doing the talking or how they're going to counteract a certain dispute or resolution.

Certainly, we all need to be thinking ahead—thinking on our feet—so that we're ready to respond when someone is done talking, but listening with the intent to speak isn't really listening at all. In fact, you could miss some very important details if all you're doing is thinking how to respond. If you do not master the art of listening with the intent to hear, you will never be a good listener and, what's worse, will never master the new winning business etiquette.

You need to focus on how you hear and receive what the individual is trying to tell you. In corporate America, I've learned that the less people talk, the more they say. Have you ever had a boss who screamed and shouted? Have you ever worked with a drama queen who was always using exclamation points? Have you ever dealt with a verbal bully, crisis addict, "drama mama," or "talk-a-holic" who never quite shuts up? Those people may talk a lot, but they don't really say much.

By contrast, when someone who doesn't say much finally speaks, others listen. Often that person has taken the time to listen to what everybody has to say, to listen to all sides of the story, to spend quiet moments paying attention to the details so that when that person is ready to participate, he or she finally has something vital to say.

Listening is not just about scoring points or getting one over on the speaker. True listening is about actually hearing what that person has to say so that you can then do something with the information you've learned. Nothing says consummate corporate executive more than being a good listener who responds appropriately and thoughtfully most of the time.

You: The Ultimate Presentation

Etiquette is how people see you and how you present yourself. Listening says a lot about how you present yourself, as does dressing appropriately. When you listen and dress appropriately, you send the following messages:

- I care
- I pay attention to details
- I can keep up
- I can do two things at once
- You matter
- This job matters
- My career matters
- The customer matters

In fact, everything you do speaks volumes. When you dress appropriately for work, it sends the same message as being a good listener.

When you show up on time (or, preferably, early), when you remember a team member's birthday (and not with a belated card), when you groom yourself properly (every day, not just when the boss is back in town), when you say appropriate versus inappropriate things, and when you are serious about your work (all the time), you show a certain sense of style and sophistication that is hard to beat. In short, you show *you*.

On the other hand, negative images of you are twice as damning because they're so hard to forget. When you are late, when you forget a team member's birthday, when you ignore details, when you rarely groom yourself or dress poorly, and when you insult people and are loud and obnoxious you send the following messages:

- I am more important than anybody else
- My time matters more than yours
- I don't care enough
- Your opinions don't matter
- The work is all that counts
- Team members are just here to help me

You matter; how you look, act, talk, groom, and dress yourself matters because they are all part of the presentation known as you.

Be careful of the messages you send and how they are perceived. Remember to embrace a sense of style and sophistication that is the best possible representative of you.

Deliver the "Authentic" You

As you think about how you present yourself and what image you're trying to project, it's important to be real about who you are. Remember, it's important that the image you're projecting is actually the person who you are.

This is where style, substance, and, in some cases, sophistication come in. Not every suit works for everybody; not every style works for everyone. Style means your style, not somebody else's. Consider the following questions:

- How do you present yourself?
- How do you articulate who you are, from the way you dress to the way you talk to the way you carry yourself?
- How do you behave in certain situations?
- How do you present yourself when your back is against the wall?
- How do you react when you're working against assigned timelines and there's a lot of pressure to deliver?

Many people in corporate America have either style and no substance or substance and no style. I think you have to have both. Successful leaders in corporate America are people who have style *and* substance.

- Style is your outer presentation: your dress, speech, grooming, manners, listening skills, and all the other outer things that represent you the minute someone sees you.
- Substance is what you bring to enhance your style, or what is inside of you that you bring to the table. If you dress nicely but have no manners, you're only half as valuable as someone who dresses and acts well. If you're a good listener but put your foot in your mouth when you finally speak, how much substance do you really have?

An executive's image is very important, and to succeed, an executive must have both style and substance. For instance, style doesn't mean dressing exactly like everyone else but dressing appropriately for the job. If the executives wear suits at your company, then wear a suit that reflects your style—maybe it's a certain color, fit, or style that works for you. But don't stop there. The suit is only the opening presentation. It's what you do when you walk into the room—the ideas you have and how you verbalize them—that sends the message that you have substance as well.

What Does Winning Mean? The Four Keys to Winning

Winning—or, succeeding—doesn't just happen. A lot goes into winning for you and for your company. In fact, over the years, I have identified four keys to winning.

The First Key to Winning: Define What Winning Means to You

Earlier you defined what "best" means to you, and in the process, you discovered how important it is to visualize what you want in order to help you achieve it. Winning is no different.

Before you can actually win, you must first define what winning feels like, looks like, sounds like, *is* like—for you. Create a clear picture in your mind. Focus on the specifics. Make sure it inspires you and represents an accomplishment.

So let's say winning for you is about increasing your department's productivity by 10 percent. It may not be the stuff of ticker tape parades or Nobel prizes or *Time* magazine covers, but depending on the size of the department, the current productive rate, and dozens of other variables, that specific goal could have a huge impact on your company.

Now think about how that might look in real life, in real time. Increased productivity will have a huge impact on this economy. More work productivity means more revenues, higher salaries, a higher standard of living, and lower unemployment. *That* is winning, and it's all doable because you've defined what winning looks like.

Following are some other great winning strategies:

- Adding one more sale per week
- Adding one more productive hour per day
- Answering *all* new e-mails by the end of the week
- Finishing a project one week before deadline
- Completing a project 5 percent under budget
- Making all hiring decisions by end of quarter

Notice that none of these winning strategies is particularly far reaching, overarching, or particularly dramatic, but all are achievable, definable, doable, and completely realistic. If you achieve every one, or just one, it will have a dramatic, legitimate, and measurable result that will demonstrate your green impact for the company.

The Second Key to Winning: Pick the Right Talent

The second key to winning is having the right talent on your team. You have to pick the right people, the best talent available, and coach and develop them in order to help yourself succeed. You have to practice having a sixth sense when it comes seeing beyond a person's résumé and external appearance to peer into his or her ambition, willingness to help, and secret passions for doing a good job. Knowing what interests people helps you to motivate people.

Are the people you're hiring special, unique talents who will work smart—and hard—to help you achieve your goals? Or did you decide to bring them on board because they were the first available or the cheapest?

Picking the right people saves time and money and increases productivity. At GCI, we have an amazing team, including a former CFO of a publicly traded company; partners from Coopers and Lybrand, PriceWaterhouseCoopers, and Accenture; VPs from Sprint and Xerox; a person who formerly helped head up innovation at 3M, one of the most innovative companies in the world; and a former executive from AT&T.

We've built a successful company from scratch, landed a huge contract, created a dynamic business model, and differentiated ourselves from every other company in the world that is focused on innovation because we have the right people in the room.

Of course, picking the right talent is only one part of the "talent equation"; now you have to coach and develop these people. The right people can become the wrong people if they don't understand their job or, for that matter, don't understand what winning is. When the right people come into the job for the wrong reasons, get frustrated because of lack of leadership, or even find themselves bored because they're not being challenged enough, they can grow stagnant.

Think about how running water flows. The ocean is always flowing. But when you stop letting water run, and it just sits there, it creates a phenomenon called water stagnation.

Stagnant water can become a major environmental hazard. So this water that was once healthy—flowing and helping things grow— suddenly becomes dangerous; it's an incubator for bacteria and other parasites. Your people work the same way.

Once you stop the flowing water of coaching and development, the once-talented employees who give life to the organization lie dormant, and instead of being healthy and vital, they become stagnant and even dangerous when they become a breeding ground for bad behavior picked up by other employees and spread throughout your company.

Development is a skill that is underappreciated by too many of today's corporate leaders. As vice president of organizational development at Motorola, I implemented one of the biggest development initiatives that was ever created at that company.

The intent there was to create mastery levels that would help develop the efficiencies, skill sets, or core competencies for management throughout the 120,000 employees in the company.

The system established mastery levels 1 through 4. In each mastery level, there were four modules, for a total of 16 modules. Each module was about four hours each, so it would take a person two days to get through one mastery level.

We wanted to ensure that we were building a particular set of core competencies not just to execute the strategies of today, but for growth opportunities for the future. So we had our leaders complete programs like change management modules, which consisted of managing in a complex, global environment.

We had our leaders complete the managing innovation and managing matrix relationships modules, which were very instrumental in helping to develop not just the businesspeople themselves but also in helping develop leaders in all countries throughout the world.

So winning is not just a short-term goal or strategy but a long-term investment in developing yourself and your team to succeed today, tomorrow, and for many years to come.

The Third Key to Winning: Innovation as the Problem Solver

Innovation, at its best, solves problems. Restaurants are in existence because people get hungry. Aquafina exists because people want purified water. And Dell exists because people want to communicate more efficiently through computers.

When you think about innovation this way, it will help you create a concept or process that differentiates your product, that makes something better, or that creates something new. You may have the answer to your city's needs, this country's needs, or even the world's needs. Innovation generates new streams of revenue. Innovation inspires. It transforms the environment.

In short, innovation is the ultimate problem solver. So how do you innovate? Better yet, how do you create a culture of innovation? At GCI, we have an innovation in enablement practice. In this practice, we analyze seven parts of a company:

1. The leader's way of thinking
2. Current team culture
3. Leadership organization
4. Team design
5. Planning process
6. Business process
7. Team effectiveness

We then determine if each of these areas is an innovation enabler or an innovation antibody. If, for instance, there's an effective, strong leadership that encourages new approaches, then leadership would be an innovation enabler. If leadership is authoritative and completely process-driven, then leadership would serve as a leadership antibody.

We then put the company through an enablement program to turn these antibodies into enablers, and create an overall culture that supports and inspires innovation. Is innovation only for technology companies to create the newest gadget? No. All companies need to innovate. Analyze what you're offering and how you offer your services and ask yourself this question: Is this the best offering in the world? If it isn't the best, then there is an opportunity to innovate.

Allow the competitive spirit in you to always want to do better. Never get complacent. Complacency is the giant killer in corporate America. When corporations get complacent, they lose their competitive edge, and they lose their will to be number one.

Plain and simple, the definition of insanity is if what you're doing isn't working, and you keep doing it. If you keep walking into a brick wall, eventually you're going to start bleeding. The answer isn't to run at the brick wall harder, but instead to use innovation to figure out a way around, under, or over that brick wall.

At www.corporateclimb.net, we have put together a series of courses to help you learn how to innovate at your job. (Read more about the many opportunities offered at the website in this book's Epilogue.)

The Fourth Key to Winning: Doing Things the Right Way
The fourth key to winning is doing things the right way. I'm in business to win. However, I'm not in business to win at any expense. I don't want to win and leave a bunch of bodies behind.

I'm not interested in treating people unfairly. I'm not interested in egos getting in the way. When you say, "This is just business" or "This is just a transaction," you demonize the entire process, and that makes it easy to cheat, easy to run over people, and easy to put people down to get ahead. While that may work in the short term, it isn't going to pay in the end.

Consider again what happened at Enron. These particular corporate executives wanted to win at any cost, and they did win—if only for a very (relatively) short time. In the process of winning, however, they ended up costing people millions of dollars in investments and lifetime earnings. One day, people's entire savings were gone—poof! just like that.

I made the decision, as a leader, that whether it be the companies we create or the employees I manage, I would always have a "people first perspective." I believe that regardless of who we're dealing with, at what level, and at which company—or even personally, especially personally—when you approach things from a people first perspective it positively enhances your relationships and, what's more, people remember that.

In the spring of 2009, my agent posted a note on my Facebook page that I was headed to Philadelphia. Suddenly I had old friends, classmates, and colleagues contacting me. That means a lot. It means that I must have made some positive impression on them. I believe that the reason so many old friends, acquaintances, and colleagues—some of them from years ago—were popping out of the woodwork to get in touch on Facebook was a direct result of making them a priority every chance I got.

And that's the kind of impact you can have when you follow the fourth key to winning and do things the right way.

Action Plan for Corporate Winning

This chapter began with a frank discussion of your definition of what corporate winning looked like to you. Now personalize that definition in the space provided below. This will help you win more effectively, more efficiently, and more personally.

My definition of winning:

_____

_____

_____

_____

_____

_____

_____

_____

_____

_____

_____

Rule #9

It's Not Just About Getting to the Top, But How You Play the Game

I N ALL THINGS, BE TRUE TO YOURSELF. YES, THERE ARE games to be played and politics to be won at the corporate level; it's not called the "rat race" for nothing. But the only way to recognize yourself at the end of the race, when you're finally sitting in that corner office, is to stay true to yourself along the way.

Achieving goals is great, but how did you do it? Did you do it by stepping over people? Do your values align with the company's? A lot of people are willing to get success at any cost these days; that's not a good strategy.

Enron, Worldcom, Blackwater, and the scandal surrounding Bernie Madoff have contributed to a long list of C-level executives who left plenty of bodies in their wake, but their actions have caught up to them now and what do they have to show for it but bankruptcy, scandal, and, in more than a few cases, a jail cell?

You want to win, but you don't want to win at any cost. In other words, don't leave a trail of bodies in your wake. As an entry-level or mid-level staffer, you should be involved in community. Be a good corporate citizen and mentor, coach, and invest in people. Some of my most rewarding experiences have been the professional accomplishments I've achieved on the job.

One could say that the general perception of executives is that they're greedy, all they think about is themselves, and they're willing to do anything that's necessary, including unethical things, in order to stay at the top. If that's your perspective, you won't be at the top long because all money isn't good money!

But take a closer look at the executives who were leading one of the biggest companies in the world, Enron. Not only did they fall hard, but they also made it miserable for thousands and thousands of employees who trusted them, who put their family's lives in their hands.

So in considering doing things the right way, understand that as an executive or someone owning or starting your own company, you will be put in positions where you have to make tough decisions.

I believe that good leaders not succeeding is not the outcome from not having the information to make the right decisions—it's the result of not making the right decisions.

They *Can* Handle the Truth

Facts should always drive a leader's decision. However, sometimes people misconstrue the facts because the pressures from analysts and shareholders to make money sometimes leads people to fudge the numbers.

Corporate America is a breeding ground for corruption. When millions of dollars in profit, loss, or corporate worth are on the line, many people will do anything—not just the right thing, but *anything*—to make sure they're on the winning end of the equation.

Leaders who will do anything will cut corners, fudge figures, forge documents, lie, cheat, and steal to get to the top. But that's no way to become the consummate corporate executive.

The message we get from daily headlines about fallen corporate leaders couldn't be clearer: doing the wrong thing is always the wrong move. Not only will you not get away with it, but it only leads to false gains and eventual loss. As a future leader coming to corporate

America, you have an obligation to do the right thing from a moral, values, and ethical perspective.

Transparency is key to doing the right thing, but many leaders assume that the less their employees know, the better off they are. In fact, one of the things I've learned in corporate America is that most leaders think employees cannot handle bad news. They're wrong.

Employees can handle tough, bad news; they usually already suspect it, if not downright know it. What employees can't handle, and where you lose employees' faith, is when you, as a leader, decide to not tell the truth or be transparent.

So I encourage you to do the right things from the very beginning of your career, and doing the right things the right way *always* starts with your being transparent, telling the truth, and taking the tough decisions to your employees and helping them understand why you had to make those decisions.

Employees may not always agree with you, but they *can* find it easier to live with the decisions you've made while you're being open and honest with them better than if they find out you lied.

Don't Leave Bodies Behind

The people who are willing to do whatever's necessary in order to achieve success will lie, cheat, and steal and leave thousands of employees wondering how they are going to take care of their family or pay their mortgage or their medical bills.

Corporate executives aren't just in charge of paperwork and spreadsheets, profit and loss, productivity and performance, but people. Leadership—true leadership—requires that not only must you produce profits but you must also produce a work environment in which people are as valuable as money.

"Leave no bodies behind" means you can't forget the human factor of leadership. This isn't always easy, but I've seen it done by some of the best, and frankly, they make it look easy.

Corporate executives are often tempted to fudge numbers, shift blame, take credit, or burn bridges in an effort to stay on top, but when you follow the nine rules in this book you don't need to do wrong—because you'll always be doing things right.

You have to respect people, you have to treat them right, you have to bring them along with you, and you have to build strong teams that respect and perform for you. Those are the true secrets to fault-free leadership.

Pull Somebody Up

Many leaders think that getting to the top is the pinnacle of their career; I say it's just the beginning. Now the real work starts, and now the fun really begins!

Your responsibility as a consummate corporate executive or the leader of a startup is to help others in need of your assistance—not as a full-time job, not at the expense of your job, but as part of your job. Remember: all of us got a helping hand somewhere along the line. Maybe it was your parents helping pay for your MBA, maybe it was that one boss who always gave you the overtime when you really needed it, maybe it was the one interviewer who took pity on your being late and let you have a second chance.

Make helping others a commitment that will help you stand out as a leader by pulling someone else up whenever you can. It might be writing a letter of recommendation, being a Big Brother or Big Sister, coaching a sports team for disadvantaged youth, or volunteering for the Special Olympics.

Regardless of what you do, who you help, and how often you do it, you owe it to the next generation of consummate corporate executives to help them out the same way someone helped you out.

Action Plan for Playing the Game the Right Way: Pull Someone Up

There are many wonderful examples of corporate giving, including the Bill and Melinda Gates Foundation, the Newman's Own company, and many others, but you don't have to donate millions to charity to pull somebody up.

Instead, you can make more personal, intimate decisions that reflect the real you. Here are just some of the many ways helping pull someone up might play out for you:

- If you were sponsored, you can look for someone else to sponsor.
- If you were mentored, you can look for someone else to mentor.
- Write a letter of recommendation.
- Offer to teach a course at a local university, college, community college, or high school.
- If you are active in sports, you can help start a team for underprivileged youth.
- You can establish a scholarship fund for a local university, college, community college, or high school.

Bonus Chapter

More Money on Your Way to the Top

W HEN IT COMES TO SUCCESS, YOU CAN'T *NOT* talk about money. And when it comes to corporate America, in general, and becoming a consummate executive, in particular, it is *not* wrong to get all you can get.

After all, no matter if you would be willing to work for free or not, you simply can't do so in these modern times. And no sane boss would ask you to—not because it wouldn't save a bundle, and it would, but because smart bosses know that employees who are properly compensated will work twice as hard as those who are disgruntled because of their compensation package.

My Thoughts on Executive Compensation and Compensation in General
My Philosophy: "You Get What You Ask For"
So, let's take a moment here to talk about executive compensation and how to structure a deal that works for both you and the company. Today's compensation packages are about wealth creation. It is not about just making a buck today but creating wealth for tomorrow, and one big way to do that is to ask for stock options so that your investment in the company is truly exponential. Remember, this is an executive compensation package with luxuries to which entry-level

employees, management, or even people in supervisory positions will not be entitled. Consummate executives not only expect stock options but demand it; in fact, they are more interested in restricted stock options than anything else because that is guaranteed money.

When negotiating the compensation package, a little outside advice from your sponsor, trusted colleague, or valued mentor is helpful. You need to know what others in your capacity make—how much, how often, and why—so that you can ask for, and get, the same. Knowledge truly *is* power in this case, so be sure to be armed with enough knowledge to argue your case if there is any blowback.

This chapter won't provide negotiation strategies or compensation scripts, but my final word on demanding an executive compensation package is that you get what you ask for. Maybe you won't get everything you want—executives love to negotiate—but how will you know if you never ask?

This is where knowing your worth, via your X-Factor, comes in handy. Those who believe in themselves, who are confident and self-assured, and who know *why* they are confident and self-assured, fare much better when discussing compensation than those who are insecure or uncertain or who waffle about percentage points.

The beauty of the system is that by the time you get to the level where you're talking executive compensation packages, you're at the point where it's often just as profitable to walk away, or, in this case, to be hired away by a competing company, as it is to demand compensation points from an unwilling or unable board of directors. Knowing this fact going in could be half the battle of coming out on top!

Creating Additional Revenue Streams
Outside Corporate America

Before beginning the discussion of additional revenue streams outside of corporate America, consider the following questions:

- What would happen if you didn't get that first job?
- What would happen if you lost out on that big promotion?
- What would happen if you got a pink slip, a rejection letter, or were laid off?

These days, in corporate America, there are no guarantees. Regardless of whether you get all the points you asked for in your executive compensation package—but especially if you didn't— you need to think about creating other revenue opportunities for yourself.

This doesn't necessarily mean you should have two jobs, but maybe you take a class at night, learn a new skill, listen to or hang out with your entrepreneurial friends, and get attached to ideas and opportunities that could provide avenues for additional revenue streams outside of work.

In other words, in the same way you use your energy and enthusiasm to propel yourself forward at work, use some of that energy and enthusiasm to secure your own financial future.

This suggestion is not intended to add extra burdens to your plate, but chances are if you are the least bit excited by turning your X-Factor into extra money, an extra job, or a whole new career, you have already thought along the lines of creating additional revenue streams for yourself.

Maybe you're considering selling items on eBay, writing a book, investing in a franchise, or becoming a silent partner in the new business venture of a spouse, neighbor, sibling, or friend. Whatever the case, associating with like-minded, entrepreneurial people will help all involved benefit from mutual relationships.

Successful people never rest on their laurels—they are always moving forward, always crossing another finish line, and always crossing off one goal to help them reach another. Similarly, why shouldn't you be preparing for you own future as an adult?

Epilogue

It's a Long Way to the Top—
Starting Your Corporate Climb

AS THIS BOOK CONCLUDES, I WANT TO THANK YOU for joining me on this journey to the top. No matter how close you are to becoming a consummate corporate executive or an entrepreneur extraordinaire or how far away that auspicious feat may feel at the moment, these nine rules will find you in a better place than you were when you started.

I admit, it wasn't always an easy journey for me; but neither will your journey to the top be effortless, easy, or even painless. I've had to endure some tough lessons along the path, but I'm wiser and stronger as a result of those lessons. Now more than ever, corporate America demands tough people doing tough jobs in tough times. I know you're up to the task, though, or you wouldn't have hung in this long.

I applaud you for getting this far, and I wish you the best in the rest of your travels. Keep reading, keep seeking, keep testing yourself, and keep pushing yourself, and you will get to play the game at the top, because that's exactly what it takes to get all the way there.

Remember that no one makes it to the top alone, and you should bring as many people up with you as you can. Not only can you trust the people who come along with you because they were there in good times and bad, but the more consummate corporate executives you bring along with you, the less room there is for those who would get to the top at any costs.

Flex schedules, a global workforce, and opportunities for entrepreneurship, intrapreneurship, and even home offices all hold great possibilities for those who would embrace and master these new methodologies in the thoroughly modern workplace.

Remember that people don't get to the top without defining what, exactly, the top means for them. Be specific and crystal clear about the goals you visualize, and go after them with gusto and a goal-oriented plan. Not everyone gets to play at the top, but those who do always get there via a specific skill set and careful, rigorous, and constant planning.

Finally, covet the destination but don't ignore the journey. Not only will what you learn along the way make you a better executive and person once you get to the top, but if you don't take time to enjoy the process along the way, you will find yourself regretful and disappointed once you finally get there.

It's kind of like closing your eyes as you travel cross-country on a bus or a train: what's the point of taking the journey if you don't look out the window and see the sights along the way?

Now, I'd be remiss in ending this book without additional means of continuing your corporate climb. In fact, this book will end with a direct lifeline to additional lessons, excerpts, words of wisdom, and dozens of resources to help you on your way to the top.

It's called www.corporateclimb.net, and I've designed the website to be your personal lifeline on the way to the top:

Don't Become a Victim!
Join the Consummate Executive Movement!
Corporate Climb is where people with high potential meet the path to advancement to become a consummate executive. At Corporate Climb, we teach high-potential entry-level and middle-management

individuals how to play the game at the top by providing a number of courses geared toward teaching everything that a college degree program doesn't. This is your stop for career advancement, the executive corporate training to get you to the top of the game.

I have designed this curriculum specifically for corporate climbers like you. In fact, the Corporate Climb team and I have put together an amazing program to get you ready to advance your career, to ascend to the top and stay there.

Here you will find additional courses to supplant the knowledge you've learned in this book. You can take three expert levels of courses:

- How to Play the Game 101
- How to Play the Game 102
- How to Play the Game 103

There is also a course on Laws of Leadership and another course on innovation. I regularly call on my colleagues, friends, and mentors to join me as guest presenters for my regular tele-seminars. At the site, you can find out more information on these teleseminars as well as the Consummate Executive Institute, where entry- and mid-level employees can receive training on how to play the game at the top.

Sign up today at www.corporateclimb.net to learn more.

About the Author

PRIOR TO FOUNDING GLOBAL CONSUMER INNO-vation, Fenorris Pearson served as vice president of consumer innovation for Dell, Inc., the thirty-third largest company in the world, with revenues of more than $60 billion, where he had the responsibility for more than 300 employees in Europe, Asia, and the Americas. While at Dell, Pearson proposed several new concepts with revenue potential ranging from $300 to $500 million. Pearson was also responsible for creating the strategy for Dell's first organization in the consumer business that was responsible for creating new products or services that derived from the understanding of human factors and human frustrations, determining what things were missing in consumers' lives, and then turning those frustrations to solutions. His group was charged with creating products driven by the consumer and not from the engineering or technology labs. Also, while at Dell, he was responsible for creating a culture of innovation for the consumer business to help transform that business from an operational excellence business model to one focused on a product leadership culture and mindset.

Before joining Dell, Pearson served as vice president for global organizational development for Motorola, Inc., a global telecommunications leader with revenues of more than $40 billion.

While at Motorola, a *Fortune* 50 company, he worked with top leadership to lead the reorganization of a $27 billion business. Pearson also lead the realignment of the product development process or front-end planning process to focus the delivery of the world's number-one–selling (in units) cell phone of all time, the Razor. He also defined and delivered Motorola's first high-performance framework with the purpose of building sustainable performance and organizational capability. His responsibilities encompassed major strategic acquisitions, process reengineering efforts, and development of the company's performance management process.

Pearson's work experience also includes positions in sales, marketing, manufacturing and distribution, customer service, human resources, and organizational development. He has a master's degree in organizational development from Benedictine University.

His lecture "How to Play the Game at the Top!" gives listeners a glimpse into the inner workings of the almost secret society that drives corporate America. In addition, Pearson helps corporations come up with fully vetted consumer-driven products. An international expert, Pearson helps corporations understand innovation through his speech "Global Innovation, What Is It and How It Impacts You!"

An avid philanthropist, Pearson currently serves on three boards: Alonzo Mourning Charities in Miami, Florida; Imagine Schools of Central Texas in Austin, Texas; and Students in Free Enterprise.

Pearson believes that, in life, "You become what you believe," and you—and no one else—controls what you make of yourself.